Also by JOHN BAILLIE

CHRISTIAN DEVOTION
THE SENSE OF THE PRESENCE OF GOD
(*Gifford Lectures*)
A DIARY OF READINGS
THE BELIEF IN PROGRESS
A DIARY OF PRIVATE PRAYER
INVITATION TO PILGRIMAGE
OUR KNOWLEDGE OF GOD
AND THE LIFE EVERLASTING

A REASONED FAITH

A
REASONED
FAITH

❖

COLLECTED ADDRESSES

by

JOHN BAILLIE

CHARLES SCRIBNER'S SONS

New York

✟ FOREWORD ✟

This collection of Addresses by my late husband is published in order that those who have read his previous writings can have access to further thoughts of his on the fun-
damentals of the faith. The Christian's interpretation of
history, the application of his faith to society, and other
Christian doctrines are here dealt with.

The Addresses were written over a large number of years,
and for a wide variety of occasions, but on issues that do
not change with time. They represent the writer's mature
mind on these subjects and were left in their finished form
at the time of his death. But, because a few of them were
written some years ago, it seemed best to make one or two
very minor changes in the text. In no case did these alter
the meaning of the writer in the least, as they were only
concerned with incidents which illustrated his thought but
which, however, dated the Addresses.

He did not write them with a view to publication, but
friends who knew of their existence were persistent in urging
that they be printed.

Once again, as in the case of the two earlier posthumous
publications, it was Dr. John McIntyre who so generously
gave of his time in selecting these Addresses from a great
number left by my husband, and in arranging them according to their contents in suitable groupings for this volume.
I am deeply indebted to him for all his kindness in the
preparation, editing, and proof-reading of this book in readi-
ness for the Press.

I would like also to acknowledge the help extended to me
by members of both Oxford University Press and Charles
Scribner's Sons during the process of publication.

F. J. BAILLIE

CONTENTS

PART I
SOCIETY AND HISTORY

1

A POINT OF LAW:
WHO IS MY NEIGHBOUR?

But he, willing to justify himself, said unto Jesus, And who is my neighbour? ST. LUKE X, 29.

How very like a lawyer! we say. We think we could have guessed that the man who asked that question was a lawyer, even if we had not been told. Anybody else would have found the word neighbour plain and clear enough, but lawyers seem to find nothing clear until they have decked it out in long rigmaroles which for all who are *not* lawyers only serve to make it ten times more obscure. In the book of the law it stood written, "Thou shalt love thy neighbour as thyself." Christ had made that law His own, saying, "This do and thou shalt live." But the lawyer, before doing it, first demanded a definition of the word neighbour. How like a lawyer!

Ah yes, but that is not the whole of the story. For behind this question there was something more than the over-scrupulosity and pernicketiness of a lawyer's mind. There was a much shabbier and more generally human motive. He wanted, we are told, to *justify himself*. "But he, willing to justify himself, said unto Jesus, And who is my neighbour?" Moffatt's version gives, "Anxious to make an excuse for himself"—which is exactly the meaning. Plainly the lawyer's pedantry was on this occasion drawn into the service of an uneasy conscience. He may not have known precisely all that was involved in loving one's neighbour as oneself, but he had an uneasy feeling that it involved something difficult for which he was not prepared. So he *wanted* the word neighbour to be an obscure word; he *wanted* it to be difficult to decide exactly to whom it was supposed to apply. At this point, then, we begin to recognise *ourselves* and to wonder whether after all this is simply a story against a lawyer. I think the truth is that we can all be lawyers when it suits us. When we are anxious to justify ourselves, you and I seem to know all there is to know about justice and we can spin out long rigmaroles enough. We can beat any jurist at periphrasis when we are anxious to get round our duty. It was *Punch* who said recently that "Many of us employ all our creative ability in thinking out words for those qualities in ourselves which we call by their usual names in others." If a commandment is unsavoury to us, we are almost sure to persuade ourselves that its meaning is obscure and its terms of reference uncertain. That we should, generally speaking, love our neighbours as ourselves we find it impossible to deny, but if there is some particular neighbour whom we do not want to love, then it is a great help to be able to boggle about the exact definition of the word. Oh no, this is not a story against lawyers, it is a story against you and me!

But you may say that none of *us*, and nobody ever again, can be in the position of the lawyer who asked this question, because *his* asking the question led at once to the answer being given for all time. Our Lord did not evade the lawyer's question, disingenuous though it may have been, but supplied the necessary definition, and supplied it in the way that lawyers love, by giving judgment in a particular case—the case of a certain criminal assault on the Jerusalem-Jericho road.

That is quite true. The word neighbour has been defined for us by our Lord's teaching, and not least by this parable, in a way that it had never been defined before. That lawyer may have been able to say with some degree of truthfulness that it was uncertain who were supposed to be included among one's neighbours, but now you and I can never say that again. Neighbour literally means a person who is nearest you; it is simply "nighboor"—the boor or fellow who is nigh you; and the question in this lawyer's mind was as to how near to you a man must be in order to be a neighbour and come within the terms of this law. Must a neighbour be a fellow-countryman, for instance, or was a Samaritan a neighbour to a Jew? This wonderful story told by Jesus supplies the answer. "Which now of these three was neighbour unto him that fell among the thieves? And he said, He that shewed mercy on him." My neighbour, then, is *whoever needs my help*. There is nobody who *may* not be my neighbour. The Jews had no dealings with the Samaritans, yet in this case the Samaritan was neighbour to the Jew.

That was our Lord's reply and it was in line with all His teaching. Indeed one might say that the more precise definition, and in fact the extension, of neighbourliness was our Lord's one constant concern in His declaration of the Father's will. Man is by nature a social animal, and the love of his neighbour is in some sense natural to him. No normal human being is a pure individualist. Everyone of us has his own circle of cronies to whom he is attached by certain ties of fellowship. Or rather he has several concentric circles. There is first the inmost circle of my own family, and to that my attachment is greatest of all. But

I have also a wider circle of friends who mean a very great deal to me, and especially, I think, the friends of my youth —"the men who were boys when I was a boy"; I do not need to be commanded to love them. And then I have a strong fellow-feeling for a much wider circle—for the men of my own race and blood, for Scotsmen in general and indeed for all good citizens of the British Commonwealth. "Greater love hath no man than this, that a man lay down his life for his friends"; yet most of us would lay down our lives without hesitation for our country and fellow-countrymen. Oh yes, if the word neighbour be taken in its ordinary common-sense meaning, then most of us can say with truth that we love our neighbours; and, if willingness to die for them be taken as the acid test, many of us can say with truth that we love them even as ourselves.

And yet all this did not satisfy Jesus Christ. To it all He would only say, Do not even the Gentiles the same? His desire was to lead us on from this mere natural neighbourliness to something altogether higher and more difficult, to what can only be called a *super*natural neighbourliness. Indeed we might say, translating a phrase of Friedrich Nietzsche's, that He so reinterpreted the word neighbour as to make it include not only the *nigh* boor, the man who is nearest to us, but also the *far* boor, the man who is furthest away from us. He did this in at least three ways. First, He insisted that, if we are to possess the highest Christian neighbourliness, we must be prepared to transcend the principle according to which our inmost circle consists of our own next of kin. "If any man come to me, and hate not his father, and mother, and wife, and children, and brethren, and sisters, yea, and his own life also, he cannot be my disciple." Secondly, as in this parable of the Good Samaritan, He taught that not only our fellow-countrymen are our neighbours, but men of other countries too, and all

men everywhere who have need of our help. Thirdly, He
taught that the word neighbour in its Christian meaning
must include our enemies quite as much as our friends, and
those whom we naturally dislike and who dislike us quite
as much as those whom we naturally like and who like us.
"Ye have heard that it hath been said, Thou shalt love thy
neighbour, and hate thine enemy. But I say unto you, Love
your enemies . . . For if ye love them which love you,
what reward have ye? do not even the publicans the same?
And if ye salute your brethren only, what do ye more than
others? do not even the publicans so?" "Sinners also love
those that love them."

Such, then, is the supernatural ideal of neighbourliness
which Christ set before His followers. And that this ideal
has powerfully influenced the Christian conscience, there
can be no doubt whatever. You and I are aware of our duty
towards those who are far from us in a way that would have
seemed impossible to the men among whom our Lord lived,
and we feel a friendliness towards them that would then
have been hardly imaginable. We have broken down the
old barriers of race and colour. We have developed a new
sympathy towards oppressed races and oppressed classes.
How our hearts, for instance, went out towards the conquered people, and how the hearts of many of us go out
towards the poor and underprivileged of our own land! How
eager we are to help them! And again, how the attitude of
many of us has changed towards our enemies! Many of us
are Christian pacifists, and even those who are not pacifists
in the full and extreme sense of the word have—or think
we have—a very different feeling in the matter from the old
warlike temper. When we read in the *Scotsman* of wars and
rumours of wars, most of us are genuinely distressed and
horrified, where our fighting forefathers would rather have
been stimulated to bellicose mutterings. So that we think

we have learned this lesson of Christian neighbourliness.
We think we come off pretty well when judged by our
Lord's standard. We think that this most testing of all
Christ's commandments is a test that we are well able to
meet.

But ah! if we think thus, it is because we do not understand the exceeding deceitfulness of sin and do not know
the wickedness of our own hearts. We think we are ful-
filling Christ's commandment because we feel no enmity
towards those who are far away from us. Yet that, after all,
is not where the rub comes. It is really quite easy to feel
friendly towards those who are far away and with whom
we stand in no active relationship. The Jews hated the
Samaritans, not because they were far away, but because,
being different in race and religion, they were so inconven-
iently near at hand. After all, then, the high and difficult
neighbourliness which our Lord demanded of His followers was not that they should love those who are far away
but that they should love those who, while far away from
them in natural sympathy and relationship, were near them
in responsibility and duty. And which of us can give a good
account of himself when it comes to that?

Take for instance Christ's command to love our enemies.
What did Christ mean by enemies? We think perhaps of
some sinister figure, some "smiler with a knife under his
cloak," who goes about seeking our life in payment of some
ancient grudge; and we feel that our consciences are quite
clear, for we have no such enemies. Or perhaps we think
of some foreign nation that threatens the security of these
shores; and some of us will feel virtuous even then, because
we refuse to feel belligerent towards any foreign nation.
But when Jesus spoke of enemies, He meant rather those
with whom we actually find it most difficult to get on.
Perhaps if every time I find the word enemy in the Gospels,

I read instead "he who is temperamentally most incompatible with me," I would really be reading the passage as it ought to be read; and then do you think my conscience would be clear? Loving one's enemies is something infinitely more difficult than just the profession of pacifist principles.

Or take again Christ's command to love all men. We think we do that when we call ourselves humanitarians. But, after all, humanity is fairly easy to get on with in the abstract, and surprisingly difficult to get on with in the concrete. There have been many great believers in the brotherhood of man who were remarkably bad brothers inside their own homes. There have been many great lovers of humanity with a big *H* who have sadly failed to love the particular specimen of humanity with a little *h* that decorated their own firesides. There have been champions of the rights of womanhood who have denied the most ordinary politeness to their own wives. There are some men who are horrified to read of the persecution of the Jews and who are nevertheless persecuting their own next of kin. This is the acid test before which even so great a man and so great a humanitarian as Tolstoy seems to have failed. Here is one among the many passages I might quote from that unpleasantly revealing document, his wife's diary: "I am bored at always being left alone. He expresses his love for me by automatically kissing my hand, and by doing me good instead of evil. . . . He disgusts me with his People. I feel he must choose between me and his beloved People." Well, the great reformer of society didn't manage very well the little bit of society that was nearest him, did he? That is perhaps why it is said that no man is a hero to his valet. What is the use of professing noble sentiments for great causes and distant objects when we withhold even the most elementary courtesies from our own wives and husbands? "He was an English gentleman," I read the other day in a novel, "and as such had obligations. But these obligations, like those of many English gentlemen, ceased at his own fireside. He, like many of us, was apt to forget that wife, sister and daughter are nevertheless ladies to whom deference is due."[1] I suppose the classical example of this in English literature is that of Mrs. Jellyby in Dickens' *Bleak House*. Mrs. Jellyby, you will remember, devoted her whole life and energy to the education of the natives of Borrioboola-Gha on the left bank of the Niger in Central Africa. She had never seen a native of Borrioboola-Gha; she managed the charitable enterprise from her house in London which also contained Mr. Jellyby and a whole brood of young Jellybys whom she had brought into the world. But while the natives of Borrioboola-Gha were being educated, the young Jellybys were not being educated, they were not even being washed, they received no upbringing. The house in Hatton Garden was a pigsty littered with papers, the children were little savages and Mr. Jellyby was a forlorn and broken-spirited man. When Caddy Jellyby, her daughter, became engaged to be married to young Turveydrop, and wished to bring the young man to see her mother, "Caddy, Caddy," said Mrs. Jellyby, quite weary of such little matters, "then you must bring him some evening which is not a Parent Society night, or a Branch night, or a Ramification night. . . . When I tell you that I have fifty-eight new letters from manufacturing families anxious to understand the details of the Native and Coffee Cultivation question, this morning, I need not apologize for having very little leisure." And Caddy went out, weeping bitterly.

In this way, then, there are at the same time revealed to us the exceeding highness of Christ's commandment and the exceeding wickedness and deceitfulness of our human hearts. If Christ tells us that the Samaritan is our neigh-

[1] H. S. Merriman, *From One Generation to Another*.

bour, then we shall exercise charity towards the Samaritan and straightway withhold it from those of our own household. And when the sinfulness of this is pointed out to us in turn, then we shall be tempted to tell ourselves that charity not only begins at home but may after all safely end there, and the Samaritans—and the natives of Borrioboola-Gha—will once more be forgotten. Yet it was the same Lord who, when His mother and brothers desired to speak with Him, said, "Who is my mother? and who are my brethren? . . . . Whosoever shall do the will of my Father . . . . , the same is my brother, and sister, and mother"; and who nevertheless in His last agony, as He hung on the Cross, took thought for His own mother's welfare, and commended the care of the blessed Lady to His beloved disciple, saying to His mother, "Woman, behold thy son!" and to the disciple "Behold, thy mother!" He was but acting on His own principle. "These ought ye to have done, and not to leave the other undone."

"But he, willing to justify himself, said unto Jesus, And who is my neighbour?" And Jesus' reply was that *any* man is my neighbour, be he Jew or Samaritan, be he near at hand or far away, if he has any need of any help that I can give. The late Bishop Gore once said a beautiful thing. He said that Christian love meant reading statistics with compassion. Let each of us then search his own heart that he may know his own unneighbourliness, and let us all pray God for grace to make us better neighbours than we have ever been before. "Search me, O God, and know my heart: try me, and know my thoughts: and see if there be any wicked way in me, and lead me in the way everlasting."

2

THE UNITY OF MANKIND

Neither pray I for these alone, but for them also which shall believe on me through their word; that they all may be one; as thou, Father, art in me, and I in thee, that they also may be one in us: that the world may believe that thou hast sent me. And the glory which thou gavest me I have given them; that they may be one, even as we are one: I in them, and thou in me, that they may be made perfect in one: and that the world may know that thou hast sent me, and hast loved them, as thou hast loved me. ST. JOHN XVII, 20–23.

In the list of Christian doctrines there is one which does not often explicitly appear, namely the doctrine of the unity of mankind. Nevertheless this is one of the fundamental doctrines of the Christian religion, one of the fundamental conceptions which Christianity has contributed to the process of human thought. All the world knows that Christianity teaches the unity of God, but the world does not so clearly understand that it teaches at the same time the unity of man. Yet in truth the two doctrines are as closely interdependent as it is possible for two doctrines to be. The unity of man can neither be established in theory save as a corollary of the unity of God, nor be realised in practice save on the basis of a common worship. And on the other hand, the unity of God can never be properly understood, but must remain as a remote and speculative dogma, until it is brought into intimate relation to this other thought of the unity of the human race.

The Christian teaching, in this as in other things, rests very clearly upon the foundation of the Old Testament. Everybody knows how largely we owe to the Old Testament the thought of divine unity, which we call monotheism, but not all realise how largely the thought of human unity derives from the same source. The Hebrews conceived of the whole human race as a single family, symbolising this conception in their legend of all mankind being the progeny of a single original pair, Adam and Eve. There were the Semites, the Hamites and the sons of Japheth, but the ancestors of these were brothers in a single household. "And the whole earth was of one language, and of one speech." "And the Lord said, Behold, the people is one, and they have all one language"—until confusion of tongues overtook them in the building of the Tower of Babel. This confusion of tongues, and the division of humanity which it symbolised, was always regarded by the Hebrews as a most tragic situation which could never be set right until, when all men again united in the worship of the one true God, the broken unity should once more be restored.

This does not mean, of course, that the Hebrews were the only people who had any feeling for the unity of the human race. I do not think they would have claimed this for themselves. There is no reason why they should not have allowed that some recollection of mankind's original unity had persisted in the minds of the sons of Ham and of Japheth as well as among their own particular branch of the sons of Shem. Actually, I suppose the fullest realisation of the unity of mankind found anywhere outside the Hebrew tradition was among the Stoics of Greece and Rome; and it is remarkable that there also it appeared as a corollary, not certainly of a true monotheism—because the Stoics continued to speak of the gods in the plural—but at least of a certain impersonal unity in the divine ordering of things. The Stoics liked to describe the universe as "one great city of gods and men."

On the other hand, it is true that not even the Old Testament has the last word to say either about the unity of God or about human unity. For that the world had to wait for the New Testament. So often in the Old Testament we seem to have what scholars call monolatry rather than monotheism, that is, rather the concentration of worship on a single God than the conviction that there *is* no God but one. And while in the second half of Isaiah and elsewhere there is a clear looking-forward to the restoration of mankind's broken unity in the worship of the one true God, yet it is only in the New Testament that this outlook becomes dominant and a way opened up towards its realisation in practice.

If in the New Testament we seek for a single passage which might serve us, by itself alone, as the charter of human unity, I think we shall find it in these words of St. John's Gospel which I have taken as my text. They are part of the great prayer of consecration which our Lord offered at the conclusion of His Last Supper with His disciples, and before setting out for Gethsemane and Calvary. In that prayer He prays first for Himself, then for the little band of His original disciples whom He was now about to leave, and finally He adds, "Neither pray I for these alone, but for them also which shall believe on me through their word." In this third part of His prayer Jesus was therefore praying for all of us, for you and me, and for all the men of later days whom, through His first disciples and through you and me, His words would reach.

And what is His prayer? It is that *we all may be one*. In

this final hour before His passion that is the concern lying most heavily on Christ's heart for those who should come after. He prays the Father that the lost unity of mankind may be restored in the fellowship of His own followers down the ages. And we should pay particular attention to the reason which He attaches, repeating it twice. It is "that the world may believe that thou hast sent me." This means that the new unity which Christ brings to mankind, the unity realised in the Christian fellowship, is the most convincing evidence the world can have of the divine character of Christ's mission. And has it not in fact been so? Has not the life of the Christian fellowship been in every age the principal advertisement of the truth of the Christian faith? Aye, but at the same time, and by the same token, has not its defectiveness been the principal stumbling-block? It is becoming clearer every day that in the eyes of the world nothing is more damaging to Christ's cause than the lack of unity within His Church. More and more does our denominationalism become a millstone round our necks. Yet even more damaging than our unhappy denominational divisions are the secular divisions, the barriers of nationality and race and class and party, which we allow to invade the Christian fellowship, making a mockery of the unity it professes to enjoy.

It was the Apostle Paul who, "as one born out of due season," realised the full implications of this Christian unity more fully than any of the original Twelve. To his mind it was clear, as it was not to some of the others, that the first great barrier to be overcome was the Jewish exclusion of the Gentiles. Addressing the Gentiles in Ephesus he writes: "But now in Christ Jesus ye who sometimes were far off are made nigh by the blood of Christ. For he is our peace, who hath made both one, and hath broken down the middle wall of partition between us . . . . that he might reconcile both unto God in one body by the cross, having slain the enmity thereby; and came and preached peace to you which were far off, and to them that were nigh [that is, the Jews]. For through him we both have access by one Spirit unto the Father."

It is, I believe, impossible to overestimate the influence which this new-found unity in Christ has exercised upon the development of human thought within the last two thousand years. It has often been pointed out by historians that the unity of Western civilisation, which perhaps reached its first complete expression in the mind of Charlemagne, was a direct derivative from the unity of the Church catholic; but it is equally clear that the unity of the Church was a direct derivative from the idea of the unity of God. This means that such ideas as we now possess of the unity of mankind have their basis in monotheism, and that no such ideas could have arisen within a polytheistic culture. The same thing I believe to be true of the modern idea of the unity of nature which lies at the root of Western science; though that does not concern us here.

Yet it is equally important to realise that these results did not flow, and could not have flowed, from Hebrew monotheism until it had been revitalised in the light of Christ's advent. The Jews did indeed clearly know that mankind was one in the divine intention, but until Christ came they found no way to make it one again. I take it as plain historical fact that such hope of a recovered unity as our Western world has entertained derives not from the Jewish idea of the unity of God, but from the Christian idea of His triunity. "That they all may be one," Christ says in His prayer, "as thou, Father, art in me, and I in thee, that they also may be one in us"; and again, "that they may be one, even as we are one; I in them and thou in me, that they may be made perfect in one." This is the unity of

Father, Son and Holy Spirit, and at the same time the participation of Christians in that unity. This is the new kind of unity which, after their Lord's departure from their earthly company, the first disciples experienced in the Upper Room at Pentecost. This is the unity which St. Paul preached to the whole known world when he proclaimed that "There is neither Jew nor Greek, there is neither slave nor freeman, there is neither male nor female; but all are one in Christ Jesus." It is that unity of the Spirit which again he described so eloquently as "one body, and one spirit . . . one Lord, one faith, one baptism, one God and Father of all, who is above all, and through all, and in you all."

Since the idea of the unity of mankind was reintroduced by Christianity into the Western mind, other patterns of unity have been entertained and experimented with, especially within the last century and a half. Other cementing agencies have been proposed, other centres of convergence than the common worship of the Triune God. Even when it has been realised that a common life must find its centre in a common worship, it has been felt that some fusion of all mankind's various creeds and worships provided a more reasonable basis of unity than the demand that all should find their way to Bethlehem and Calvary, and to that Upper Room in Jerusalem where on the first Pentecost "all they who believed were together" and "were baptized" and "devoted themselves to the teaching of the apostles, and to fellowship, to the breaking of bread, and to the prayers." For the modern mind, which has its own preconceptions as to the course which history should follow, is very loath to believe that the enlightenment and salvation of the whole world should be by means of a revelation vouchsafed to a single obscure people in an outlying part of the world at one particular time in what is now the distant past. This is the loathness which the philosopher expressed when he wrote that "The Absolute loves not to pour the whole of its essence into a single instance."

Not only, however, were it better that we should take history as we find it, but the strategy implicit in this divine ordering of things is not wholly hidden from us. Had God willed to reveal His salvation separately to each individual, or to each separate race or nation, then all could have found God without at the same time finding one another; and the broken unity of the race would thus not have been restored. But since He has so ordained things that men can find salvation only by betaking themselves to one place; by listening to the same old, old story; by being received into the one fellowship; by reading in the same book; by praying the self-same prayers in the self-same Name; by being baptized with the same baptism and partaking of the same sacred Meal—"all made to drink into one Spirit," as St. Paul has it; and by drawing their whole spiritual sustenance from the same unbroken tradition handed *down* from age to age and *across* from one nation to another;— in so ordaining things God has done all He could do, short of altogether abrogating the freedom of human choice, to bring us together again in the restored unity of the human family.

"All they that believed were together," we read of the first little company of Christians in the Upper Room; and "they devoted themselves . . . to the breaking of the bread," in repetition of the Supper which the Lord had eaten with His disciples before praying this prayer. "All made to drink into one Spirit," says St. Paul. Throughout all ages this eucharistic action has been the solemn seal and symbol of Christian unity, and I believe it to be literal truth that it has done more than anything else for the cause of human reunion generally. And our Lord Himself willed that it should be so. "Do this," He commanded, "in remembrance of me." And now, in closing, I shall take leave to read you a page from a recent work of English scholarship:

Was ever another command so obeyed? For century after century, spreading slowly to every continent and country and among every race on earth, this action has been done, in every conceivable human circumstance, for every conceivable human need from infancy and before it to extreme old age and after it, from the pinnacles of earthly greatness to the refuge of fugitives in the caves and dens of the earth. Men have found no better thing than this to do for kings at their crowning and for criminals going to the scaffold; for armies in triumph or for a bride and bridegroom in a little country church for the proclamation of a dogma or for a good crop of wheat; for the wisdom of the Parliament of a mighty nation or for a sick old woman afraid to die; for a schoolboy sitting an examination or for Columbus setting out to discover America; for the famine of whole provinces or for the soul of a dead lover; in thankfulness because my father did not die of pneumonia; for a village headman much tempted to return to fetish because the yams had failed; because the Turk was at the gates of Vienna; for the repentance of Margaret; for the settlement of a strike; for a son for a barren woman; for Captain So-and-So, wounded and prisoner of war; while the lions roared in the nearby amphitheatre; on the beach at Dunkirk; while the hiss of scythes in the thick June grass came faintly through the windows of the church; tremulously, by an old monk on the fiftieth anniversary of his vows; furtively, by an exiled bishop who had hewn timber all day in a prison camp near Murmansk; gorgeously, for the canonisation of S. Joan of Arc;—one could fill many pages with the reasons why men have done this, and not tell a hundredth part of them. And best of all, week by week and month by month, on a hundred thousand successive Sundays, faithfully, unfailingly, across all the parishes of Christendom, the pastors have done this just to *make* the *plebs sancta Dei*—the holy common people of God.

To those who know a little of Christian history, probably the most moving of all the reflections it brings is *not* the thought of the great events and the well-remembered saints, but of those innumerable millions of entirely obscure faithful men and women, every one with his or her own individual hopes and fears and joys and sorrows and loves—and sins and temptations and prayers—once every whit as vivid and alive as mine are now. They have left no slightest trace in this world, not even a name, but have passed to God utterly forgotten by men. Yet each of them once believed and prayed as I believe and pray, and found it hard and grew slack and sinned and repented and fell again. Each of them worshipped at the eucharist and found their thoughts wandering and tried again, and felt heavy and unresponsive and yet knew—just as really and pathetically as I do these things. . . . The sheer stupendous *quantity* of the love of God which this ever repeated action has drawn from the obscure Christian multitudes through the centuries is in itself an overwhelming thought. (All that going with one to the altar every morning!) [1]

The lost unity of mankind;—is there any hope of restoring it in another way than this?

[1] Dom Gregory Dix, *The Shape of the Liturgy*. Dacre Press: A. & C. Black, Ltd., London, 1945, p. 744 f. Used with permission.

3

HOPE AND DISENCHANTMENT

*When they therefore were come together, they asked of
him, saying, Lord, wilt thou at this time restore again
the kingdom to Israel? And he said unto them, It is not
for you to know the times or the seasons, which the Father hath put in his own power. But ye shall receive
power, after that the Holy Ghost is come upon you: and
ye shall be witnesses unto me both in Jerusalem and in
all Judaea, and in Samaria, and unto the uttermost part
of the earth.* ACTS I, 6–8.

THE outlook of our Western nations is at the present waver-
ing in the most uncertain way between hope and despair.
In the time of my youth we were all cheerful optimists who
believed that everything was getting better and better all
the time. Eagerly we

> dipt into the future, far as human eye could see,
> Saw the vision of the world, and all the wonders
> that would be . . .
> Till the war-drum throbb'd no longer, and the battle-
> flags were furled
> In the Parliament of man, the Federation of the world.
> And passionately we believed that
> Better fifty years of Europe than a cycle of Cathay.

We regarded human history as a tale of continuous progress,
and we believed that in our own twentieth century the
tempo of this progress was going to be marvellously stepped

21

up, so that the brave new world of our dreams was now very near at hand. Today there are still many among us who cling to this belief. They are impressed by the vast increase of power which advancing science is putting into the hands of mankind, and they feel assured that mankind has sufficient good sense and sufficient good will to employ this power in the service of the highest ends. Yet there are as many or even more who now feel quite differently. It may be that our remaining Utopians are only the rear-guard of the nineteenth century, representing the last flickerings of the fire that still burned so brightly in my youth. This seems to be evidenced by the fact that there are more of them among my own grey-haired contemporaries than there are in the younger generation, and more also among the intellectually second-rate than among the leaders of thought. But among the youth of our Western nations, and in the books of many of our most penetrating writers, optimism has largely given way to disenchantment. The gloomiest forebodings are now in fashion, and in many quarters a spirit of hopelessness has begun to take possession of men's minds.

In these circumstances it is well that Christians should consider what guidance their Christian religion has to give them in this whole matter of hope and despair. And this guidance is nowhere more clearly indicated than in the words I have just read from the Acts of the Apostles. We are here told by St. Luke that when Jesus appeared to His apostles after His death, they put this question to Him: "Lord, will you at this time restore the kingdom to Israel?" That was the form which hope had long taken among the Jews. They looked forward to the establishment of an independent Israelite monarchy after being delivered from the foreign yoke. The restoration of the kingdom was understood by many in a political sense, as it is among the Zionist

Jews to this day. But it was always understood in a spiritual
sense also; and in the teaching of the great prophets the
political aspiration had largely given place to a spiritual one.
The promised king was to be no mere earthly ruler, but
the Messiah sent by God for the final salvation of His
people and through them of the whole world. The apostles
were convinced that Jesus Christ was this promised Messiah.
Their hopes had indeed been severely shaken by His cruel
death on the Cross, but when after three days He appeared
to them again, hope rose once more so high as to prompt
the question whether the Kingdom of God was not now
to appear in its full glory without further delay, whether
Christ was not at this time to restore the kingdom to Israel.

John Calvin writes in his commentary that this question
has as many errors in it as words—*totidem errores quot
verba*. He thinks the apostles were still conceiving the
Kingdom of God in a political sense, and the phrasing of
their question certainly gives us this impression. But even
if the restoration they had in mind was no merely national-
ist one but the dawning of an era of final blessedness for all
mankind, their question showed how little they had taken
to heart what their Lord had been at pains to teach them
during the years of His ministry. So in the answer He now
gives them, He reminds them what that teaching was.

His answer is as follows: "It is not for you to know the
times or the seasons, which the Father has kept within His
own authority. But you shall receive power. . . . , and you
shall be my witnesses. . . ." You will notice that this answer is in two parts. In the first part is a warning against
false hopes, in the second against an equally false despond-
ency.

Let us take the two parts separately.

Jesus had again and again warned His disciples that they
must not attempt to assign any date for the appearance of

the promised Kingdom of God. He said He did not know the date Himself. "But of that day and that hour knoweth no man, no, not the angels which are in heaven, neither the Son, but the Father only." And this He now repeats when He tells them that it is not for them to know the times and the appointed seasons, which the Father has kept within His own authority. That was the answer the first Christians got when they wanted to forecast the course of future history, and that answer is as valid for us today as it was for them long ago. It is not given to you and me to know the long-term strategy of God. He has kept that within His own authority. The final end of history is indeed assured to us. Its end is in a glorious consummation such as eye has not seen nor ear heard neither has entered into the heart of man to conceive. The end of history will be the glory of God. But when it will come about, or in what manner, or by what stages, or if indeed at all by stages, we are not informed. Any forecasts we make are made at our own risk and peril, and the exigency in which the mind of our Western nations now finds itself is largely due to the fact that for many generations past it has been fond of taking this risk, which has now turned out to be a bad one. It has made belief in the almost automatic progress of mankind into a central article of its faith. It has been full of Utopian illusions about the promise of the future. Frequently it has been lured by promises that the Golden Age was very close at hand, just round the next turning as it were, and capable of being established, some said by swift and sudden revolution, others by a somewhat more slowly evolving legislative reform.

In one of his books Jacques Maritain expresses his amazement at discovering how much the nineteenth century, which at first sight seemed to be an age of positive knowledge, was really an age of prophesying. And somewhere else I recently read the remark that our own age puts the palmiest days of Ahab quite in the shade for the number of false prophets it has produced. We have for long been accustomed to laugh at those who from time to time have claimed foreknowledge of the date of the end of the world and of Christ's second coming. We have rightly judged them to be the victims of superstitious ignorance. Yet we ourselves have often been superstitious in another way, putting an equally superstitious trust in the gradual evolution of human nature, in the omnipotence of science, and the salvation of mankind by the advance of scientific knowledge. Therefore no less than the quaint folk who watched the skies for Christ's second coming, we need to be reminded that it is not for us to know the times and the seasons. We too need to be told that the time is not yet, that we are living in an evil world in which we are nevertheless called upon to do our daily duty in obedience to our Lord's command, while we wait in hope for that which is to come.

But now let us attend to the second part of Christ's answer to the apostles' question: "But ye shall receive power when the Holy Ghost has come upon you, and ye shall be witnesses unto me. . . . unto the uttermost parts of the earth." I have said that the intemperate optimism in which we had so long indulged is now taking its revenge upon us. The tide of events in our own lifetime has expelled these false hopes from the minds of large numbers of our contemporaries, and especially from the minds of the rising generation, and often leaves literally nothing in their place. The belief in inevitable progress was an ill-founded belief, yet it is sad to see it disappear when it leaves men without any spiritual anchorage at all. How many young men and women in how many countries of Europe today are literally without hope! I spoke to many such during my visits to Germany after the end of the War. Hitler had promised them his *tausendjähriges Reich*, his grand new order that

was to last for a thousand years. They know now how utterly without substance that promise was, and they were
left with nothing to live for, with no belief in the future,
with nothing before them but dull despair. Among ourselves things are not so bad as that, but they are bad enough.
There is a growing uncertainty of direction, a growing fear
of the future, a growing lack of confidence and trustfulness
as we face the business of living.

What we need then is to listen to the second part of
Christ's answer, the part introduced by the word "But."
"It is not for you to know the times and the seasons, *but*
ye shall receive power . . . . and ye shall be my witnesses.
. . . ." This promise of power was the promise of the de-
scent of the Holy Spirit at Pentecost, and the rest of the
chapter shows us that the promise was redeemed without
delay. The disciples found that after their Lord's disap-
pearance from their midst, they still had to go on living
in the same old evil world, and today we are still living
in it. They had still to wait, and to wait indefinitely, for
the glory that was to be. But they were not left in de-
spondency. They were not left in despair. They were not
left to let their hands hang idly and listlessly by their sides.
On the contrary they were filled with zest. They were filled
with hope. They were filled with joy—and with faith and
love. Are there any books in the world so full of hope, so
full of joy, so full of faith and love, as the books of the New
Testament, which were written by these same men and
their immediate associates? And the reason was that they
had received power—the power of the Pentecostal Spirit
—and they proceeded at once to rely upon this power and
to use it to the glory of God.

Now what I so often find wrong with our mind and mood
today, what I find wrong with so many of the books being
written by those who are influencing the mind of youth,

is that they lack this New Testament sense of the power of the Spirit. It is as if, being disenchanted of our Utopian illusions, we were now ready enough to accept the first half of our Lord's sentence, but had not yet stayed to listen to the second half of it. Yet if that should be true of us, then our last state is worse than our first.

When I turn from such books as these to the New Testament, two things impress themselves upon my mind. On the one hand the New Testament writers have their eyes wide open to the limitations of our human situation in the present evil world. They know the desperate corruption of the human heart. They know that the powers of evil are still rampant in the world about them. They cherish no illusions about human perfectibility or inevitable progress. They never confuse Christ's eternal Kingdom with the kingdoms of this world. But on the other hand they all declare that the advent of Jesus Christ and the gift of the Spirit at Pentecost have marked the dawn of a new age, a glorious age, an age in which all sorts of things are going to be possible that were not possible before; and they enter into this new age with eagerness and confidence and with a wonderful sense of the power now at their disposal. This, they felt, was a time in which it was good to be alive. "Blessed are the eyes which see the things which ye see," Jesus had said; "For I tell you that many prophets and kings have desired to see those things which ye see, and have not seen them; and to hear those things which ye hear, and have not heard them." "The darkness is passing," writes St. John, "and the true light is already shining." "We are being transfigured from glory to glory," writes St. Paul, "Therefore, if any man be in Christ, it is a new creation; old things are passed away; behold, all things are become new."

That was the temper of St. Paul as he set about to cover the whole known world on his missionary journeys. None understood better than he how corrupt was the heart of man, and how powerful the forces of evil in the world in which he had to live. None was ever further from cherishing any illusions about the forward march of mankind. But he had been given a work to do, and power to do it. And such a work too! Christ had said here: "Ye shall be my witnesses. . . . . unto the uttermost parts of the earth." St. Paul took that command quite literally, and believed that the power of Christ was sufficient for its accomplishment. He even seems to have believed that the whole known world might be evangelised within his own generation, the leaven of the Spirit of Christ penetrating even to the pillars of Hercules and the gates of the Western seas.

The condition of the world today is indeed not such as to justify any light-hearted Utopian expectations, yet in many respects it is a far better world than that in which the first disciples found themselves, when their Lord was taken up out of their sight. The doors of Christian opportunity are far more widely open to us than they were to them. Christ had then only a few score of possible witnesses in the world, but now, apparently, He has over eight hundred million—for that, according to responsible sources, is the number of people who now profess and call themselves Christians. How bright a prospect would then be ours, if we Christians of today were as ready to use the resources at our disposal as was that first brave little band, realizing as they did the power that had been given them, and showing a like eagerness in our witness! Then indeed we might be able to sing with truth:

> Uplifted are the gates of brass;
> The bars of iron yield;
> Behold the King of Glory pass!
> The Cross hath won the field!

4

REWARDS

Verily I say unto you, They have their reward.
ST. MATTHEW VI, 2.

This phrase appears three times in this chapter of our Lord's discourse. It is here in verse two, and it is repeated in verse five and again in verse sixteen. It is a saying to which perhaps we have never given sufficient attention, and I propose that we should think of it today.

Jesus is here instructing His disciples in the practice of piety. He speaks separately of three aspects of that practice —almsgiving, prayer and fasting—but He makes the same point with reference to them all. When you give alms, He says, do not sound a trumpet before you, as the hypocrites do, so that men may praise them. They have their reward. No, when you give alms, do not so much as let your left hand know what is in your right hand to give. Keep your almsgiving secret, and God who sees what is done in secret will give you your reward. Again, when you say your prayers, don't do it at the street corners, as the hypocrites do in order that men may see them at their devotions. They have their reward. You go into your room and shut the door, where men will not hear you. But God will hear you, and you shall have your reward from Him. Finally, when you fast—that is, when you have decided to discipline yourself in some way for a season—don't look dismal like the hypocrites who go so far as to disfigure their faces, so that men may notice they are fasting. It is enough that God knows it. He will see to your reward.

"They have their reward," says Jesus in all three cases. That is to say, they have got what they wanted, what they set out to get. When the hypocrite paraded the streets, distributing his largesse and trumpeting his progress as he went, it was not really the poor he was thinking of, but his own reputation as a benefactor. When he said his prayers, he was seeking not so much a response from God as a response from men. What he wanted was the reputation of being a devout person. And again when he fasted, it was for the sake of making a good impression. Well, says Jesus, no doubt he did make a good impression. No doubt he did gain a wide repute as a devout person and as a philanthropist. In all three cases he got what he wanted. His account is settled. "He's had it," as we say in our contemporary slang. And nothing more is coming to him. "Take heed that ye do not your alms before men, to be seen of them; otherwise ye have no reward of your Father which is in heaven." Had the man's real concern been for the glory of God and the granting of the graces for which he prayed, he would have got these things. God who sees in secret would have given them to him, as He will give them to all who seek them with their whole hearts.

You may perhaps think the picture of the hypocrite somewhat overdrawn. Most men's motives are mixed. The philanthropist has some real concern for the poor but he wants the reputation too. Many people go to Church both in order to satisfy public opinion, or perhaps as an example to their children, and in order to devote themselves to better things. Even so, however, our Lord's warning might still stand. Our getting will be according to our seeking. If we only half want to draw near to God, we cannot expect to get very close to Him. If we only half want His peace in our hearts, we cannot expect to have much of it. Nevertheless we must be very careful not to cheat our consciences in this matter. It is in this very context, in this very chapter, that Jesus says, "If your eye is not sound, your *whole* body will be full of darkness. . . . No man can serve two masters. . . . Ye cannot serve God and mammon." When the worldly motive is present at all, it has a terribly corrupting influence upon the heavenly one. So often it is the worldly motive alone that is really effective to action; so that I have to ask myself, for instance, "Would I really have gone to Church this morning if somebody else's opinion of me did not at all come into account?" If not, then I must admit that my neighbour's good opinion is my sufficient reward.

Now I have myself often been struck by the fact that so many people get what they want or something very like it. There are of course also many people who seem to get nothing. There are large numbers of men and women in the world today whose overmastering desire is only for a handful of rice and who cannot even get that; and everywhere there are those who, by reason of ill-health or accident or, it may be, a native deficiency of wit, are denied even the paltriest of the goods for which they seek. Nevertheless I am impressed by the number of people who succeed in the things into which they have really thrown their energy. The voluptuary who wants a life of sensual satisfaction can usually get it. How many men have wanted money before everything else and, just because they have given their whole minds to it, have amassed a fortune! Others have wanted only power, and have succeeded in ruling their little roost, whatever else they may have missed. While still others have concentrated, like the hypocritical Pharisee of whom Jesus speaks, on being well spoken of, and men have indeed spoken well of them. But the word which our Lord speaks about them all is a terribly tragic one. "They have their reward." They've had it. Greek scholars have pointed out that the word Jesus here uses (ἀπέχω) was the word commonly used in New Testament times on forms of receipt. It is as if these men were made to sign a receipt saying: "Paid in full. I have received all that is due me. My account is settled." There is nothing more coming to them. Not for them the "purer light" or the "calm and heavenly frame." Not for them the secret recompense or the joys of the heavenly Kingdom. Nor can they possibly complain. "Seek, and ye shall find," said Jesus; "Everyone that seeketh findeth, and to him that knocketh it shall be opened." Well, they have found what they sought; the doors at which they knocked have opened up before them. But the doors at which they have not knocked remain eternally closed. "And age comes on, uncheered by faith and hope." It is indeed a tragic sentence!

I am reminded here of some of the proposals Plato makes in his famous dialogue, *The Republic,* for the reform of society. He believes that society may be divided roughly into three classes of men corresponding to the three classes of people who were present at the great Olympic games. There were many who looked upon the games as a sort of fair or market; they came to buy and sell, and their motive was gain. Then there were the athletes who took part in the games, and their motive was to win honour and fame and reputation. Finally, there were the spectators who sought neither gain nor honour, but were content to con-template the human scene below. Now Plato's proposal was that the Republic should avail itself of this manifest difference of motive and interest that existed, and was likely always to exist, between different groups of its citizens. He believed that a stable and peaceful order of society could be obtained only if each of these classes was allowed to have what it wanted. Our modern ideas of social reform are largely concerned with the question of wealth, and they all tend towards the equal distribution of wealth over the whole of society. But Plato's strange proposal is that the men who want wealth should be given it. They would (in reasonable division among themselves) have all material property in their hands. By their buying and selling they would be supplying the economic needs of the commonwealth; but at the same time they would be getting what they sought; they should have their reward. Similarly with the ambitious class of citizens—the lovers of honour. They should not be allowed to possess property or wealth, nor should they on the other hand be given a voice in the ultimate affairs of government. They should form rather the civil service and the standing army. It is in these spheres that honours and decorations are won, so that they too will get what they want and have their reward. But the ultimate control of the ship of state should be, Plato thinks, in the hands of the third class, the contemplative class, the sages, who are indifferent alike to wealth and honour, being concerned only for the good of the commonwealth as a whole. They are to possess no property and, as to honours and decorations, it is to be a condition of their appointment that they should not want them. According to the Catholic tradition a bishop, before being consecrated, is required to say the words *"Nolo episcopari"*—"I do not want to be made a bishop." Similarly, to Plato, no man who wanted power was fit to be entrusted with it. The sages who governed would indeed have their reward, but it would be no worldly one; it would be the reward of a good conscience towards God and their neighbours.

I have reminded you of this teaching of Plato, not of course because I think his solution of the political problem is a workable one, but only because of its bearing on this matter of rewards. Plato believed that, within limits, men should be allowed to get what they want. Our Lord's point is rather that, in the providence of God, so often they do seem to get it. Therefore the question with which I am confronted as I read this page of the Gospels is, "What do I really want? What is it that I am really seeking?" Any observer of our human scene must have the impression that we are all bent on something, and seeking it with a most feverish desire. "We pine for what is not."

> There is not any hour complete,
> Nor any season satisfied.

There is no lack of zest and zeal among us, no lack of energy and eager action. There is hardly any limit to what men will do and endure, or to the sacrifices they are ready to make, scorning other delights and living laborious days, in order to get the things on which their hearts are most set. But I fear the impartial observer would be forced to conclude that most of this feverish desire was directed towards worldly wealth and worldly place and worldly power and the satisfactions of the flesh.

Well, there is an Observer. There is an impartial Observer. There is one who not only sees what is done in the market-place, at the street corners and in the synagogue, but who "sees in secret." What does He observe in me? What is *my* heart's secret dream? What is the guiding thread through all my thoughts? What is the real animating motive of all I do? Do I seek *first* the Kingdom of God and His righteousness, or do I, while not altogether indifferent to these nobler rewards, give the first place to something else? You remember the young man in the Gospels who thought he could have both kinds of reward at once. He came to Jesus seeking the heavenly treasure. Jesus told him how to attain it: "Sell what you possess, and give it to the poor; and come, follow me." But "when the young man heard this, he went away sorrowful." And Jesus, looking after him, might well have said to him, "Verily I say unto you, You have your reward." For "he had great possessions" and he was going to keep them, and that apparently was what he really wanted. His account was closed. He could expect nothing more. Not for him the "solid joys and lasting treasure" which "none but Zion's children know."

But the Observer is not merely an observer, He is also a Giver; and to those who truly set their hearts on them, these solid joys and this lasting treasure are securely promised. Where your treasure is, Jesus goes on immediately to say, there shall your heart be also; and God who sees into your heart's secret will surely give you this reward. Some may perhaps be inclined to object that "virtue is its own reward"—that the man who has eschewed worldly prizes should be quite content with the consciousness of his own integrity, and needs no Father in heaven to give him some further prize. That, however, is rather a Stoic sentiment than a Christian one. The Stoic was content with virtue, but Jesus wanted men to have something more. He wanted them to have joy—solid joys and, as another hymn says, "social joys"—in the communion of saints and in the fellowship of God.

> What social joys are there,
> What radiancy of glory,
> What light beyond compare!

Some of you will remember that the philosopher Immanuel Kant had a strong strain of Stoicism in him, and came very near to saying, as the Stoics did, that virtue itself was enough, that nothing was worth having or seeking save the dutiful will. But his Christian inheritance got the better of him in the end, making him realise that there could be no final satisfaction until to virtue was added something like joy.

It is not enough that we should set our hearts on the attainment of virtue, or on keeping the commandments. "All these things have I kept from my youth up. What lack I yet?" You see, the young man knew he lacked something. "Concerning the righteousness which is of the law," said St. Paul, "I was blameless. But what things were gain to me, those I counted loss for Christ. Yea doubtless, and I count all things but loss for the excellency of the knowledge of Christ Jesus my Lord. . . . that I may win Christ, and be found in him, not having mine own righteousness, which is of the law, but that which is through the faith of Christ, the righteousness which is of God by faith; that I may know him, and the power of his resurrection, and the fellowship of his sufferings, being made conformable unto his death; if by any means I might attain unto the resurrection of the dead." These are the things with which the Father, who sees in secret, will reward them that diligently seek Him.

5

UNACKNOWLEDGED INFLUENCE

Then asked they him, What man is that which said unto thee, Take up thy bed and walk? And he that was healed wist not who it was. ST. JOHN V, 12–13.

I HAVE heard sermons on unconscious influence, that is, on influence that men unwittingly exert; but now I wish to speak on unacknowledged influence, that is, on influence that men unwittingly receive. Here was a man whose limbs had been paralysed for thirty-eight years, so paralysed that he could not even lift himself from his pallet into the healing waters within a few feet of where he lay. Jesus, taking compassion on his distress, bade him take up his pallet and walk. This he did, and was quite cured of his infirmity. Who is the man that cured you? they asked him; but "he that was healed wist not who it was."

In this incident I find a parable of the situation in which humanity stands today. The man in this story is contemporary man, who is all the time reaping benefits of which Christ is the source but without realising who it is to whom he owes them. We who profess our faith in Christ and take our full part in the ordinances of worship do indeed constantly render thanks to Him for all His benefits, but so often we do this in very general terms and do not stop to think how many and how great these benefits are, so that very much of our debt remains in fact unrealised and unacknowledged. In spite of the weakness of its verse and of its music, we might well learn from that popular hymn which bids us:

> Count your blessings,
>   Name them every one,
> And it will surprise you
>   What the Lord hath done.

But if this is true of the professed and observant disciples of Christ, how much more true is it of the world at large! For it was the world at large that Christ came to save. His mission was to the whole of humanity. Scripture does not say, "God so loved the Church" but "God so loved the world that he sent his only begotten Son." Nor can there be any doubt that the world at large has reaped countless benefits from that mission. Think first of the kind of benefit with which this incident is particularly concerned—the healing of disease. Think of the tender care that has been lavished on sick folk, on lepers, on old folk, on undernourished children all over the world, and on Christians and non-Christians alike, under the banner of Christ's Cross and because He sent out His disciples to do these very things! Think how much of the development of the whole hospital system owes to Christian enterprise, and how different it would all be today if Christ had not devoted a large share of His time to the cure of disease, and infected the world's conscience with something of His own compassion for the sick, the halt, the maimed and the blind. The two earliest of the great modern hospitals in Britain are called by the names of two of Christ's disciples—St. Thomas and St. Bartholomew. Is it not true of many who have been cured in these hospitals that "they wist not who it was"? And do all the war-blinded service-men at St. Dunstan's remember that their patron was a follower of Him through whom many blind men of long ago were given back their sight?

Did all those who were picked up from the battlefields of the recent wars know that the red cross on the ambulance was Christ's Cross? Must it not be said of many of these that they "wist not who it was"?

Yet it is not only on the sick folk among us that Christ confers these unacknowledged benefits. It is, for instance, only when we travel to parts of the world which Christian influence has not yet effectively reached that we realise how much He has done for the recognition of the proper dignity of women. Think of that most precious of all our national institutions—the family life of the home circle. What do you think ordinary family life would be like today if St. Columba and St. Ninian had never carried the Gospel to our Scottish shores? We do not perhaps regard Charles Dickens as a particularly Christian writer, and yet how essentially Christian is his feeling for family life! Could the pictures he draws of it in the *Christmas Carol* be anything like what they are, if Christ had never lived and never died? We have recently so secularised the Christmas feast that *Punch* made somebody exclaim, when he heard a Christmas service spoken about, "I don't know what we are coming to. They are even bringing religion into Christmas nowadays." Ah, poor man, he wanted his Christmas, and he enjoyed his Christmas, but "he wist not who it was" that had given it to him.

I might speak also of how much we owe to Christ for the familiar embellishment of life in the arts that most delight us, but I shall confine myself to a single example— the example of music. Do we realise that the first beginnings of polyphonic music in our Western world were in the singing of the Christian liturgy—that it is entirely due to the influence of Christian music that we possess any harmony, any part-singing, or anything but simple melody.

But what I really want to speak of, because it is most

significant of all, is the influence Christ has exercised upon our common conscience and our accepted standard of moral values. I number among my own friends and acquaintances many men and women who do not confess the name of Christ or acknowledge His Lordship, and yet whose consciences, whose feelings, whose instinctive responses, and whose treatment of their neighbours, are conditioned by generations and centuries of Christian tradition. I do not mean, of course, that the cast of their minds or the conduct of their lives is truly Christian. That could not be, while they lacked the Christian grace of faith, for faith is the very foundation and source of the true Christian temper. Nevertheless the temper they do exhibit is such as it could not possibly have been had the culture into which they were born, and in which they have been reared, remained a pagan one—whether Nordic pagan or Roman pagan or anything else.

It was said, for example, of the Cambridge philosopher, Henry Sidgwick, who was not a professing Christian, that "he exhibited every Christian virtue except faith." How many men I have known of whom I have been tempted to say just that! And yet one is constantly overcome by the fear that such vestigial Christianity can at best be only a temporary phenomenon. Men like Sidgwick were themselves brought up in the Christian faith and in the Christian Church, and, though they have forsaken the faith, they continue to enjoy some taste of its fruits. But can they pass on this taste to their children, if they are no longer brought up within the faith? How long will the Christian temper survive among us, when it no longer receives nourishment from its original source, which was a whole-hearted commitment in love and obedience to Him who loved us and gave Himself for us, even Jesus Christ our Lord? How long will the healing influence survive after it shall come to be said that they "wist not who it was" that had healed them?

Consider also the influence Christ has exercised upon the *public* conscience of the Western family of nations. Unfortunately, one cannot say with any conviction that this influence has yet gone very far towards making the nations act in accordance with their conscience, but it has at least made their consciences uneasy. If the races and nations do not behave towards one another as they ought, they can no longer say that it is because they do not know how they ought to behave; and if they do know how they ought to behave, it is very largely from Christ that they have learned it. *Would* they know this if it had not been true that, as St. Paul says, Christ broke down the middle wall of partition (or, as we might translate it, the iron curtain); so that there is neither Jew nor Greek, Barbarian nor Scythian, slave or freeman, but all are one in Him? *Would* we have the same uneasy conscience about our present inter-racial relations as now disturbs us, if it were not for Him? Or the same uneasy conscience about war?

Alas, that so often it is only an uneasiness that we have, and not what St. Paul calls "the godly sorrow that worketh repentance"! Alas, that the pain in our minds is so often the wrong sort of pain! But such as it is, we Church folk have also to admit to our very great shame and confusion that very often this uneasiness, which derives from Christ, has led to more imaginative and resolute action at the hands of those outside the Church than at the hands of those within it. That is true of many movements in our history for the welfare even of those classes to whom our Lord gave special thought and care—the poor and underprivileged, prisoners and slaves and refugees (whom the New Testament calls "strangers within the gate"). That should be deeply humbling to us. But it is glorifying to our Lord. These indeed do not acknowledge His glory, but *we* should acknowledge that His glory is through them enhanced. These are they who will ask in surprise, "Lord, when saw we thee an hungered and fed thee? or thisty and gave thee drink? When saw we thee a stranger, and took thee in? or naked, and clothed thee? Or when saw we thee sick, or in prison, and came unto thee?" And perhaps the Lord will answer, "Inasmuch as ye have done it unto one of the least of these my brethren, ye have done it unto me." They did what He commanded, though they "wist not who it was."

Yet we may ask how this can be? How can Christ acknowledge as His own, services which have not been rendered in His name? St. Paul says, "Whatever is not of faith is sin." Can we say then that those who do the deeds of Christ without acknowledging His name, as we Church people acknowledge His name, have any kind of faith? I think perhaps St. James would reply for them, "Yea, a man may say, Thou hast faith, and I have works; show me thy faith without thy works, and I will show thee my faith by my works." Can a man have faith without knowing it? Did perhaps even Henry Sidgwick have faith without knowing that he had it? I think myself that we must allow something like this to be true, remembering the emphatic words of our Lord Himself, "Ye shall know them by their fruits." Faith as a disposition of the soul is something far deeper than intellectual assent, though where that assent is lacking it must be gravely compromised and have little power of continuance. I think then that men can have faith without knowing that they have it. Yet let me remember one thing. If I speak thus of unconscious faith, I must speak of it, not in excuse for my own unbelief, but in charity towards my neighbour's. As was most truly said by John Ker, the great Scottish preacher of last century, "There is such a thing as unconscious faith, but those who plead it in their own behalf do not possess it. With them it is conscious unbelief."

But as for you and me, we cannot say that we "wist not who it was." You and I do know, don't we, that we owe everything to Christ? When I think of my own upbringing, the love and care that were lavished on me in my youth, the kind of home into which I was born, the community in which I was reared, the gracious influences that were brought to bear on me, the examples that were held up before me, the kind of teaching I was given, the signposts that awaited me at every turn of the road, the fences that were set to keep me wandering from the way, the warnings that were given me against every pitfall, the words in season so often spoken to me:—when I think of all these things, and in spite of my shame for having so little profited from them, I must indeed prostrate myself in gratitude before the memory of my parents, my teachers, my wonderful friends, and those who wrote the books I was given to read, who rendered me this inestimable service. Yet I know that they themselves had it all from Christ. Nothing of it would have been there, if Christ had not come to seek and to save that which was lost. *I* cannot say that I wot not who it was. And I think that none of *you* can say that ye wot not who it was. Yet I fear that we still accept many things from His hand without ever stopping to thank Him. So perhaps after all I cannot better end my sermon than by saying to you again, and this time with no apologies:

> Count your blessings,
>   Name them every one,
> And it will surprise you
>   What the Lord hath done.

6

THE SHEMA

Hear, O Israel; The Lord our God is one Lord: and thou shalt love the Lord thy God with all thine heart, and with all thy soul, and with all thy might. And these words, which I command thee this day, shall be in thine heart: and thou shalt teach them diligently unto thy children, and shalt talk of them when thou sittest in thy house, and when thou walkest by the way, and when thou liest down, and when thou risest up. And thou shalt bind them for a sign upon thine hand, and they shall be as frontlets between thine eyes. And thou shalt write them upon the posts of thine house, and on thy gates.

DEUTERONOMY VI, 4–9.

MAN is a talking animal. A poet, watching the swallows gathering in the sky, may write that "The pilgrims of the year waxed very loud, in multitudinous chatterings," but no other animal is such a chatterbox as man. Sometimes, when travelling in a country whose language I did not understand, I have sat in an inn or railway compartment or wandered through a crowded market-place, when every tongue seemed to be going at lightning speed, everybody apparently trying to talk everybody else down; and I've wondered what on earth they could possibly be finding to say to one another. And it would seem that the more primitive the community, the more unimpeded is the flow of words. Savages chatter almost unceasingly. Silence is not primitive, but rather a characteristic of complex and sophisticated civilizations, being due either to diplomacy, as in the case of Count Moltke who was said to have the gift of being "silent in seven languages," or to social embarrassment—though in this case we can always, in this country at least, save the situation by falling back upon our changeable weather.

What do we talk about, you and I, when we sit at table or by the fireside with our families, or when we go out walking with them? We always find something to say, and perhaps we are inclined to think that it does not very much matter what it is. Conversation is a social function which keeps us in friendly touch with each other, no matter what may be the topics discussed. It may only be sport or the increased cost of living or the day's news or the latest movie or, as George Crabbe put it long ago,

> Intrigues half-gathered, conversation-scraps,
> Kitchen-cabals, and nursery-mishaps,

but it all helps, as it were, to lubricate our human and family relationships and keep them sweet, if it is carried on pleasantly and with good humour.

Yes, but the first question I want to put is whether conversation really *can* be kept sweet, if it remains on that superficial level. It is remarkable how easy we human beings find it to pick a quarrel with one another. Even the smallest of small talk will provide plenty of opportunity for it. Some little devil always seems to be listening in at even our most casual conversations, and it is seldom very long before he finds an opportunity of sowing discord. And to allow one devil in is to allow a whole crowd of them—the devils of bitterness and malice and jealousy, the devils of untruthfulness and slander and back-biting. St. Paul knew all about it when he wrote to Timothy about "strifes of words, whereof cometh envy, strife, railings, evil surmisings, perverse disputings."

I am sure that if we are honest with ourselves we shall all have to confess to the very great difficulty in keeping these devils at bay. The first little devil makes his entry so unobtrusively that we are far from suspecting the legion at his heels. What is it another poet says?

"Who knocks so loud?" "A little lonely sin."
"Enter," I answered; and all hell was in.

We just can't resist that barbed word, that little dig. It is such a little dig, but if it pricks and is resented, then we can't help remarking that apparently "the cap fits"; and that lets in a whole crowd of demons at a rush. While our own shortcomings are hidden from us, the shortcomings of others stand out so clearly that we can't help drawing their attention to them. Of course they pay back in kind, and since it is even more difficult to refrain from self-defence than it originally was to refrain from launching the attack, we soon find ourselves in the thick of battle.

It is in this way that family relations are poisoned. Our sentimentalities about the joys of the fireside circle and "home, sweet home" are apt to be considerably chastened by a study of the Divorce Court proceedings, and yet the vast majority of these family tragedies seem to take their rise in just such trivial bickerings. But what is true of the family is true of every other kind of social group. Nor must I, as one whose whole life has been spent in colleges, exempt the Senior Common Rooms of our universities; for I am ashamed to confess that even the shabbiest of household devils seem to find no special difficulty in slipping into them. And what of the wider circles of community? What above all of the family of nations? Don't some of the disputes at the council tables of the United Nations read exactly like the disputes round the dinner table in many a private household? It is not a different set of devils, but precisely the same set, that builds so many barriers between husbands and wives, and that forged the "iron curtain" now dividing Eastern Europe from the West.

What then can we do about it? How are we to keep these devils out? The answer is that they cannot be kept out while our relationships with one another, our walk and conversation with one another, remain on that super-ficial level. Our human predicament is so desperately seri-ous, and our human nature so desperately prone to wicked-ness, that common life cannot be kept sweet so long as it remains trivial. It is only by going deep down to the heart of things that we can find a solidarity strong enough to over-come the surface tensions; and the deep heart of things is God. Only by together laying hold of the divine unity, only by grounding ourselves on the knowledge that "the Lord our God is one Lord," can we ever master the things that divide us. We can never shut the little devils out unless we let the great God in.

Now listen again to our text. Remember that these are the words which, according to the Book of Deuteronomy, Moses spoke to the Israelites as they were about to enter the promised land of Canaan after their long desert wander-ings. They were going to adjust themselves now to the hum-drum of a steady pastoral existence after the unsettled nomadic life to which for so long they had been used, and their society would now be open to new temptations. So Moses said to them:

Hear, O Israel: The Lord our God is one Lord: and thou shalt love the Lord thy God with all thine heart, and with all thy soul, and with all thy might. And these words, which I command thee this day, shall be in thy heart: and thou shalt teach them diligently unto thy children, and shalt talk of them when thou sittest in thine house, and when thou walkest by the way, and when thou liest down and when thou risest up. And thou shalt bind them for a sign upon thine hand, and they shall be as frontlets between thine eyes. And thou shalt write them upon the posts of thine house, and on thy gates.

When you read that, do you wonder that even in this modern day we must continue to go back to the ancient East, to these rude tribesmen of three thousand years ago, and to these ancient Hebrew scriptures, for the solution of our most urgent problems? How these words touch the very heart of the matter! The only way, so these rude tribesmen are told, to keep their life sweet in their new surroundings, the only way to keep the legion of Canaanite devils out, is constantly to stay themselves upon the unity of God, and to love the one God with all their heart and soul and might. And you will notice that they are given specific guidance as to their *conversation:* "thou shalt talk of these things when thou sittest in thy house, and when thou walkest by the way, and when thou liest down, and when thou risest up"—not just in an occasional theological debate, which is so apt to become academic and unreal, but in the ordinary small talk of every day. "And thou shalt teach them diligently to thy children"—ah! that was a very important part of it. It makes us ask ourselves what kind of upbringing the little ones are receiving in many homes today. What teaching are they getting, and above all what example are they being shown? What is being laid up in their young hearts? What things have their young ears sometimes to listen to?

"And thou shalt bind these words for a sign upon thine hand, and they shall be as frontlets between thine eyes. And thou shalt write them upon the posts of thine house, and on thy gates." The Hebrew people came to take these instructions very literally—probably more literally than was originally meant. "Hear, O Israel": the Hebrew word for "hear" is *shema;* so the words which follow came to be known as the *Shema*, which to this day is recited as part of the service in every Jewish synagogue. And at morning and evening prayer every Jewish male still wears the two phylacteries, as they came to be called, one between his eyebrows and the other tied round his left arm, with these words written on them; and every observant Jewish house has a little box, containing a scrap of parchment inscribed with the same words, fixed to the post of the door.

The Shema is the very centre of Jewish piety, and goes far to explain the marvellous strength of Hebrew family life and the solidarity of the Hebrew community throughout the ages. There is more in our Christian creed than the *Shema*, but the *Shema* is a vital part of it; and we Scots, no less than the Hebrews, owe the strength of our family and community life to its having been anciently built on this foundation. What was the talk like in the Christian homes of Scotland's past? What was it like in the household of my own youth and in the other households I used to visit? We talked of fun and games and books and the happy trivialities of school and home; yes, but it was always against the background of something sterner and more profound. Our parents diligently taught us the commandments of God, often leading us back to them as we sat in the house or walked by the way, and always—*always*—when we lay down or when we rose up. Though not literally, yet none the less truly, they were bound for a sign upon our hands and as frontlets between our eyes; and they were written upon the posts and on the gates of the house where I was born. What after all would our history have been apart from this? What has Scottish history to show the world that was really independent of it? We have other reasons for reading the history of Greece and of Rome, but what other reason have we for reading either the history of Israel or the history of Scotland? I think Scotland must confess with St. Paul, "He that glorieth, let him glory in the Lord." When walking in the island of Lewis a few years ago, I happened to stop for a moment at the open window of a shed where herrings were being packed. Immediately inside the window was a machine that seemed to split and clean the herrings, and pack them into cases, all in a single operation. A young woman was tending the machine, and when she looked at me I said, "That is a wonderful machine." "Aye, sir," she answered, "the works of man are wonderful, but not so wonderful as the works of God!" Well, when I want to boast about Scotland, I tell a few stories like that; for not in every part of the world would I have received such an answer.

Are we doing for our children of the rising generation what our fathers and mothers did for us? Are we keeping this tradition green? Times change, and the superficialities of life change with them. The topics of conversation round the dinner-table are now very different from what they were in my youth. But the ultimate issues of life remain quite unchanged. "Other foundation can no man lay than that is laid, which is Jesus Christ." Most of us know that, under God, we owe everything to the influences that were brought to bear on us in early life. I have heard a man of my own generation exclaim in the course of a discussion, "Whatever you may say about Christianity, it made my mother what she was." Will our children be likely to say a thing like that about us? I can imagine no greater service we could render to Christ than that twenty or thirty years hence our children should be fortified in their allegiance to Him as often as they remember how *we* were enabled by His grace.

Yet let us not think in this matter of Scotland only. The old national frontiers count for so much less than they used to do. The world, whether we like it or not, is more and more developing into a single interdependent community; and the failure to recognise this, or the attempt to erect any kind of iron curtain between the nations, can only lead to disaster. Moreover, I believe this to be a cause for Christian rejoicing. The world is destined to become one just because God is one—because, as the *Shema* says, "The Lord our God is one Lord." Yet I think we all know that this one world will prove quite unmanageably large and cumbrous, if it does not ground itself also on the rest of the *Shema*, "Thou shalt love the Lord thy God with all thine heart and soul and might." The great peril of our time lies in the fact that the secular unity of our world is threatening to outstrip its spiritual unity. If no single nation has ever succeeded in holding together on the basis of merely economic or utilitarian interest, if every stable society known to history has owed its stability to the presence among its members of some common spiritual outlook, what hope is there for our United Nations, if it is to have no profound basis of that kind at all? That is why you and I must cease to be parochial, and give at least as much thought and prayer, as much time and as much money, to the task of world-evangelisation as to the maintenance of the Christian traditions of our own beloved land.

7

TRUTH AND LOVE*

That we henceforth be no more children.
But [that we] speaking the truth in love, may grow up into
him in all things, which is the head, even Christ.

EPHESIANS IV, 14–15.

PERHAPS this should be translated, not "speaking the truth in love, may grow up into him," but "speaking the truth, may in love grow up into him." The words "in love" may go with the second phrase instead of with the first. Either way the main point of the Apostle's advice is the same. Truth and love, he says, are both necessary, if we are to grow up into Christ. Love without truth won't do it, and neither will truth without love. Truth provides the light and love provides the heat, and both are needed for any healthy development into Christian manhood. Love will mislead us unless it be enlightened by truth, and truth will mislead us unless it be warmed by love. The reason for this is that truth is one of God's attributes and love is another, and we can only worship God aright if we worship Him under all His attributes and in the whole fulness of His Godhead. You know how often the Old Testament couples together God's truth and His mercy—and mercy is just the Old Testament way of saying love.

The whole paths of the Lord
Are truth and mercy sure

* This address was written in 1941.

To those that do his cov'nant keep
And testimonies pure.

One might say that all false religion consists in worshipping some of God's attributes to the exclusion of others.
All idolatrous forms of worship grasp something of the nature of the true God but also leave something out, and so
turn the true God into an idol of man's own making. And
of course false worship leads inevitably to false living. Love
without truth leads inevitably to sentimentality and insincerity. It is what St. Paul calls love with dissimulation and
not love unfeigned. But truth without love may lead to
equally grievous errors, and it is about these that I would
speak now.

To you and me today truth may well seem the most
precious of all possessions, and like all precious things there
is very little of it about. If the Devil is the Father of Lies,
then he would seem to be more rampant in the world today
then he has ever been before, going to and fro on the earth
and walking up and down on it. In many parts of the world
men are now being fed on deliberate lies, and truth (like
some other things) is a strictly rationed commodity. Adolf
Hitler in his notorious book elaborately and eloquently de-
fends systematic lying as one of the most important instru-
ments of totalitarian warfare, and those who have ever
listened to Lord Haw-Haw know that he is putting this
weapon to its fullest and most skilful use. When I was crossing the Atlantic, the ship's wireless operator one day retailed
to me a preposterous piece of so-called news which he had
just heard on the air from Italy; and when I asked him if
he really believed it, he shrugged his shoulders and said,
"Honestly I've come to the point where I don't know what
to believe." The propaganda, you see, was beginning to take
effect. Not knowing what to believe is but a stage on the

way to believing whatever is proclaimed most loudly and brazenly.

Speaking the truth, then, may well seem the virtue to be cherished above all others. It is one of the things we are fighting for, isn't it? We want to put truth back on its ancient throne, restoring it to its proper place in the relation between the peoples of the world. And because truth is our goal, truth must also be our weapon. We must, as St. Paul says, have our loins girt about with truth. Our hope is that if, as a nation, we go on speaking the truth to other peoples and feeding ourselves only on the truth, we shall prevail over all lying propaganda in the end.

And yet the Apostle would tell us that speaking the truth is not enough. We must speak it in love. Perhaps truth itself is not strong enough to defeat falsehood, unless it be warmly clothed in love and mercy. That is what the psalm says, "Surely his salvation is nigh unto them that fear him; that glory may dwell in our land. Mercy and truth are met together; righteousness and peace have kissed each other."

The ineffectiveness of truth without love and mercy may be illustrated from many spheres. To speak the truth to others is indeed our bounden duty, but it can be a most dangerous thing if it is separated from other equally bounden duties. There are different ways of speaking the truth, and some of them are quite disastrous, and some of them are positively wicked. I remember a man saying to me, "I met our friend So-and-So this morning and I gave him some home truths." Well, what he said may have been true, but it was certainly not said in love. It was said in anger, and I think with a spice of malice. But truth spoken in malice is little likely to convince, and that for the very good reason that it can never even be quite true. The malice must always taint and corrupt the truth, so that only truth spoken in love can ever be quite true.

Good manners consist very largely in the proper combination of sincerity and tactfulness. If I meet an acquaintance on the street who has some obvious untidiness about his dress, it may in some circumstances be my duty to call his attention to it, but obviously I must be very careful how I do it. I don't say, "You have on your waistcoat either some of yesterday's soup or some of this morning's porridge"—although that indeed may be an exact scientific description of the facts as known to me. Here is a region in which something more is required of us than scientific accuracy. But this is not only an affair of manners, it is also an affair of morals. Any action done without love is sinful, and speaking the truth without wrapping it about with love may often be very sinful indeed. Few things can work more havoc in human relationships than candour without kindliness. How many marriages are embittered by the husband who insists on telling his wife the whole truth about herself, or by the wife's devastatingly faithful and tiresomely persistent recital of her husband's shortcomings. There are a great many true things known to you and me about which we must forever keep silent, because we have not grace enough to speak them in the way in which they must alone be spoken. It is a good rule: Never speak the truth until you have learned how to speak it in love. You remember Tom Pinch's little untruth in *Martin Chuzzlewit* and what Dickens says about it:

There are some falsehoods, Tom, on which men mount, as on light wings, towards heaven. There are some truths—cold, bitter, taunting truths—wherein your worldly scholars are very apt and punctual, which bind men down to earth with leaden chains. Who would not rather have to fan him in his dying hour, the lightest feather of a falsehood such as thine, than all the quills that have been plucked from the sharp porcupine, reproachful truth, since time began?

I remember once being much impressed by a passage in one of the published letters of that great writer and most spiritually-minded man, the late Baron von Hügel, in which he spoke of the rule he kept before himself in criticising and reviewing other people's books. He said he always tried to begin his criticism by saying what he could in praise of the book, then he voiced his doubts and objections, and finally returned again to the book's good points in his closing sentences. It is a good rule, and one which I have since tried to follow in my own reviewings. Von Hügel, you see, was anxious to wrap round his candour with kindliness. He knew that mere hostile criticism would be little likely to have the desired effect. A man of spirit will bridle up against hostile criticism, and a man of no spirit will only succumb to a feeling of inferiority which will hinder rather than help him. Either way more harm is done than good. That is why so many controversies are both endless and fruitless. Mere polemic seldom does anything but stiffen the adversary's resistance. That is what is wrong, for instance, with most of the controversy between the Roman Catholic and Protestant Churches—or for that matter between any two churches. We speak truth with intent to wound rather than to reconcile and to heal.

The same thing holds when we come to speak the most important truth of all—when we come to preach the Christian Gospel to them that are without. "Is it not unspeakably sad," writes one of the finest Roman Catholic spirits of our day, Karl Adam of Tübingen, "that we Catholics are no longer, as formerly, recognized by our love, that no longer faith and love, but faith alone is our distinguishing mark? . . . . . Why are we in the works of our love no proof of the spirit and strength of the victoriousness of the Catholic faith? Why do we rather take refuge in cheap speech and in dead books to testify to our faith, whereas the only overwhelming and effective apologia for the living reality is that of the glowing heart, of active devoted love?" It is a question which Protestants also would do well to put to themselves. Have we learned to preach the Gospel in the only way in which it is likely to be received? Have we learned that faith without love is as dead in its power of testimony as in its power unto salvation? Let the words we speak be never so true, their truth is little likely to be recognised unless they are lovingly administered, and unless the truth of them is seen to bear the fruit of love in the lives of those who speak. For what is the truth which Christianity preaches? It is that God is love, and that the duty of man is to love God in loving his neighbour as himself. The Christian truth is that love is the greatest thing in the world, the essence of Godhead and the sum of human duty; but how can you expect men to believe *that* if it is preached to them in a loveless way or if those who preach it fail to show by their lives that they really believe what they say? I remember hearing of a Manchukuo woman—a sick woman carrying a baby—who was converted to Christianity through being offered a seat in a bus by a young missionary of our church. That missionary was not even speaking the truth in love—he could not do that because he had not yet learned the language; he was allowing his love to speak the truth for him!

Or let me return for a moment to the case of Germany today. The Germans, I have said, are being systematically fed on lies, and one of the objects of our policy is to let them know the truth. We are doing all we can to disillusion them now—to get something of the truth through to them; and we look forward to a day when the people of Germany will be finally disillusioned, and see Hitler for what he is, and turn their backs upon him and all his works. Well, let us not suppose that this is going to be an easy task. People don't like hearing the truth about themselves from the mouths of their enemies. How are we to overcome their distrust, their very natural suspicions? We can do it only by speaking the truth in love. We must show them that we are concerned not to harm them but to save them. I believe that after the victory our most important task, more important even than setting the occupied territories on their feet again, will be the task of setting a defeated Germany on its feet again, and restoring to the people something of their self-respect. The greatest menace of the post-war period would be a chaotic and despairing Germany. That would be a most dangerous canker right in the middle of Europe. We do not want to drive the German people, the most numerous race in Europe, into anarchy and bolshevism. Oh, it will be so tempting to let the Germans hear some home truths at the end of this war! I feel the urge to do it in myself! But it is certain that the home truths will not go home unless they are spoken in love and kindliness. It must be Christian truth that we speak to them. It must be truth not intended to crush but to evangelise. Otherwise there will be no hope of a restored order in Europe.

For we must remember once again that behind all this that I have tried to say about what we should do and should not do, there lies the very nature of the Gospel itself. Christ did not come to earth merely to tell us the truth, and if He had come only to do that, then His coming would have been of none effect. He spake as never yet man spake, yet not even *His* speaking would have been listened to, if He had done nothing else than speak. Our Lord came to earth, not to tell us what to do, but to do something for us. He did not come to give us a piece of His mind. He did not come to give us good advice. Thank God for that! Advice is cheap. The world has always been full of good advice. In some ways there is too much of it floating about these days rather than too little. But the world has always been short of loving action, and it was to engage in loving action for our sakes that our Lord came to earth. He spoke the truth indeed, but He spoke it to us from the heart of a love that suffered and died for our sakes.

In the modern world, by which I mean the world that we are trying to defend against the threat of Nazidom, the quest of truth has played a large part and occupied a very honoured place. Modern science and philosophy are informed with a most determined zeal to see things as they are—to look the facts in the face, wearing no blinkers. Why is it, then, that the quest for truth has so often seemed to lead modern man away from God instead of towards Him? I am sure it is because it has so often been pursued in isolation from other quests that are of equal importance. "Truth for truth's sake," men say; yet truth for truth's sake is not enough, any more than "art for art's sake" of which we used to hear so much. When the love of truth is artificially separated from other loves, it becomes what is called pure scientific curiosity, and pure scientific curiosity is not a thing that has any right to exist by itself. A doctor cannot be a good doctor without scientific curiosity, but he is a very bad doctor indeed if he has nothing else to mingle with it. And a philosopher cannot be a good philosopher unless the love of truth is mingled in his heart with the love of love. And the reason for this is, as I said at the beginning, that truth is only one of God's attributes, while love is another, and that we cannot be saved from an idolatrous corruption of one attribute except by loving Him and worshipping Him under His other attributes too. When the love of truth is pursued in abstraction from the other claims that life makes on us, it is more than likely to degenerate into the love of error. God in His own indivisible nature is the only reality that must be sought and loved for its own sake alone. And only in the love of God is there salvation for you and me, and for the peoples of the earth.

> To them that fear him surely near
>> is his salvation,
> That glory in our land may have
>> her habitation.
>
> Truth met with mercy, righteousness
>> and peace kiss'd mutually.
> Truth springs from earth, and righteousness
>> looks down from heaven high.
>
> Yea, what is good the Lord shall give;
>> our land shall yield increase.
> Justice, to set us in his steps,
>> shall go before his face.

PART II

CHRIST AND
HUMAN DISCUSSION

8

CHRIST AND HUMAN DISCUSSION

And he came to Capernaum: and being in the house he asked them, What was it that ye disputed among yourselves by the way? But they held their peace: for by the way they had disputed among themselves, who should be the greatest. And he sat down, and called the twelve, and saith unto them, If any man desire to be the first, the same shall be the last of all, and the servant of all. And he took a child, and set him in the midst of them: and when he had taken him in his arms, he said unto them, Whosoever shall receive one of such children in my name, receiveth me: and whosoever shall receive me, receiveth not me, but him that sent me. ST. MARK IX, 33–37.

IT IS often said that we are living today in a post-Christian situation. By this two things are meant; first, that Christianity was the chief formative influence of our traditional cultural background; and second, that, however much the world has now disengaged itself from this tradition, it can never again return to its pre-Christian state, or be as though Christ had never lived. And both these things are true. Other influences besides the Christian Gospel have gone to the formation of the European culture of the last two thousand years. The roots both of Western science and of Western art are largely in ancient Greece, the roots of Western law and government are largely in ancient Rome, and something there is we owe to the native spirit of the Northern nations; but the deepest thing in our tradition, that unifying principle which took what it wanted from these earlier cultures and fitted them, after due transfiguration, into its own new pattern—this deepest thing came neither from Greece and Rome nor from the new lands of the North, but from Judaea. And now it is true that we who came after can never again be as those who went before. The pre-Christian order of things has been destroyed by Christianity, and destroyed for ever. The world may no longer accept Christ's lead, but it cannot now be as though He had never spoken, or even as though it, itself, had never listened. Some proposals are of such a kind that if they have once been made to us, and especially if we have ever seriously entertained them, we cannot again—not even by the completest present rejection of them—be as though they had not been made. That is the world's situation today. In great part it may have rejected Christ's proposal. But in this way or in that Christ is still present in most of our discussions. They are post-Christian discussions, not merely in time but in their very substance; and our situation is a post-Christian situation.

My reason for choosing this text is that it gives a good example of how Christ first entered into human discussion —how He intervened in the great human debate. He had just begun His last journey to Jerusalem. He had been up north in what we now call Syria, and was moving southwards through Galilee, along with His disciples, before crossing into Transjordania. As they approached Capernaum, Jesus had been walking a little ahead of His disciples, as was often customary when a teacher walked with his followers. But this time they were lagging behind somewhat more than usual, and their voices were raised a little in what Jesus would at once recognize as the shrill accents of personal dispute. When they reached the houses and found shelter in one of them, their talk suddenly ceased, and then

Jesus turned to His disciples and said, "What was it you were discussing on the road, and that you stopped discussing just as I came in?" But they did not tell Him. They just could not tell Him. They were silent, the Evangelist says: "they held their peace." For what they had been discussing with each other on the road was "which of them was the greatest" or, as we might also translate it, "who was greater than who." Yet though they did not tell Him, Jesus knew, or guessed enough for His purpose. He sat down and called the Twelve around Him and spoke the famous words, "If any man desire to be first, the same shall be the last of all, and the servant of all." Then, to give point to the saying, He took one of the children of the house, and put His arm around it, and said to the disciples, "Whoever receives one such child in my name receives me; and whoever receives me receives, not me, but Him that sent me."

That was how Christ first entered into our human discussions. That is how He has entered into them all down the ages. That is how He enters into them still.

First, He wants to know what our discussions are about. We are always raising our voices over something, getting excited and using shrill tones. Some of these discussions are carried on with ourselves, in our own secret hearts and in the privacy of our own chambers. Not a day passes, and hardly an hour, when my soul is not holding debate with itself, argument meeting argument in often indecisive combat. Other discussions are carried on between one man and another, or between one group or class or nation and another; and again there is not a day, and hardly a daylight hour when our newspapers and radios do not report such discussions. Indeed in these days our newspapers and our news broadcasts contain hardly anything else. Have another look at yesterday's paper, and you will see how column after column is a report of some heated discussion or dispute, with raised voices, shrill tones, excited minds. Well, there is not one of them about which Jesus Christ does not want to know. There is not one of them to which His Gospel is not relevant, or about which He has not something to say. This is true of all the debates I hold with myself in my own mind: the Gospel of Christ, if true, would make a difference in every case. And it is true also of the public debates and disputes we read about in the newspapers—of the debates at the sittings of the United Nations, of the debates in India and in Greece, of the debates between employers and employees, of the debates about food, about education, and everything else. "What is it," Christ asks, "that ye disputed among yourselves by the way?"

"But they held their peace." It would have embarrassed them to tell Him. And how often it embarrasses me to tell Him what I have been debating in my own mind. Sometimes after such an argument with myself, the time comes for me to say my prayers. Christ would like me, I know, to bring the argument to Him in prayer, but alas! very often I don't. I just can't. When I am on my knees in His presence, I have to hold my peace about that argument I had with myself. I put it out of mind, to be taken up again only when my prayers are finished. And why do I do this? It is because I know that Christ will have something quite pointed to say about it, something that will go right to the heart of the problem, and I am often not prepared to hear that said, because I am not brave enough to face what it would involve. Isn't the same thing true of most of the public disputes reported in our newspapers? Men are not prepared to let Christ have part in these disputes. They know that if they let Him in, He would say something terribly disconcerting and disturbing. And by this time they know pretty well what it would be.

Why then is it that we are so embarrassed about letting

Christ be a party to our discussions? And why do we feel that His contribution to them would be so inconvenient and so upsetting? Clearly it is not that we think it His intention to make unnecessary trouble for us, for we know very well that what He wants to do is to help us out of our troubles. Nor can it be fundamentally because we doubt whether what He has to say is true; for if we really thought that, we should have Him in at once, and hear Him, and then refute Him; which is just what we so seldom do. No, I am afraid it is usually for very much the same reason as actuated the disciples in our story. They did not want Christ in their discussion, because they had been discussing "which was the greatest" and "who was greater than who," and because they knew that if they told Him that, He would say something very like what He did say: "If any man desire to be first, the same shall be the last of all, and the servant of all."

Now is it not true that the reason why we hesitate to bring the Gospel of Christ into most of our discussions is that we do not want this said? Go over in your mind the arguments you had with yourself yesterday, as you lay back in your chair smoking your pipe or cigarette, or as you communed with your own heart upon your bed in the night watches; go over also the public disputes recorded in yesterday's newspaper; and ask yourself from how many of them this desire to be the greatest—the most honoured, the most privileged, the most powerful, the most prosperous, the best paid, the best fed or the best housed—was entirely absent. And is it not because of this kind of element in our discussions that we want to keep Christ out of them? Is it not because we are unwilling to let our action be wholly governed by His conception of humble service to the complete exclusion of all manoeuvring for power and jockeying for place?

You may perhaps ask whether it is only Jesus Christ who faces us in our human discussions with this particular challenge. Should we not find it equally difficult to allow Socrates to have a part in them, or Lao-tze, or especially perhaps an Old Testament prophet like Ezekiel? Well, I am sure we should find that uncomfortable enough on many an occasion, and very disturbing for our complacency. Socrates would be a most awkward delegate to the council chambers of the United Nations—and not there alone. Yet actually it is not Socrates, it is not Lao-tze, that has troubled the conscience of the Western world for the last two thousand years. The burning words of the prophets of Israel have indeed troubled our consciences often enough, but that was because Christ took up their message into His own message, nowise desiring to destroy it but only to fulfil it. Yet to say that we should find even the words of the prophets *equally* disturbing is surely to exaggerate. The disciples were no doubt familiar enough with the prophetic teaching, but it had never confronted them with so radical a challenge as they now had to face in the presence of Christ. Here, for instance, is the careful comment which the distinguished Jewish scholar, the late Dr. Claude Montefiore, has to make on this very passage and especially on Christ's saying that he who desires to be first must be the last of all and the servant of all. "The saying about service," he writes, "is apparently new. The Rabbis were indeed never weary of preaching humility and its greatness. In that there is nothing new. But this combination of humility with *service* would seem to be new. Lovingkindness, the doing of deeds of charity and love, are indeed familiar themes enough in the Rabbinical literature. But I do not think I am wrong in supposing that this touch of eager, personal service, especially towards the sinner and the outcast, was a special characteristic of the religion of Jesus, and a new thing in Judaea when He preached it."

Yes, there is no doubt about it. Ours is a post-Christian situation. It is Christ who has put us in the predicament wherein we now stand. Look a little more closely at this symbolic action when He called the child towards Him and put His arm round it. "Whosoever," He said, "receives one such child in my name receives me; and whosoever receives me, receives not me, but him that sent me." They had been disputing as to which of them was the greatest, and Christ tells them that he is greatest who most humbly serves the least of his fellow men. The least does not of course always mean the children, though sometimes it does. The child was but an example, the example that was nearest to hand when He spoke, of those who most stand in need of our help. But our Lord's meaning was that if only we were ready to forget our own engrossing affairs, our own swelling ambitions, our desire for personal advancement and all our pride of place, and asked ourselves instead how we can be of most use to the neediest, weakest, poorest, most suffering of our fellow-creatures, then we should be manifesting something worth calling greatness. In the true scale of values, the values of the Kingdom of Heaven, that man is first who is the humblest servant of the last and least.

"Whoever welcomes one such in my name, welcomes me," said Christ, with His arm round the child. Christ wants us to do these things for His sake and in His name. He wants us to help the starving children of Europe for His sake, and the starving adults too. And for His sake He wants us to give more thought to getting a sufficient ration for them than to getting a more generous ration for ourselves. Perhaps somebody will say that it does not much matter whether we do these things in Christ's name or not, so

long as only we do them. Ah, but that is not true! It matters enormously, not only that we should feed the starving
babies of Central Europe, but that we should put something of the love of Christ into the feeding of them, and
not mere expediency—to avoid possible repercussions upon
our own future prosperity. And hear again the generous
words of Montefiore, the Jew: "The dynamic effect of
this saying has been enormous. All social service wrought
in Christ's name and spirit is wrought to him. Who can
measure or count the deeds of sacrifice and love to which
this saying has prompted?" It is in the name of Christ that
these things have been done for the last two thousand years.
Do you think they will continue to be done at all, if we
now forget His name?

Finally Christ adds, "And whoever receives me, receives
not me, but him that sent me." There would be no special
significance in our reception of Christ, if in receiving Him
we were not at the same time receiving God. But just as it
is true that when we sink all private ambition in the service
of the lowliest of our fellow men, it is really Christ whom
we are welcoming into our minds and lives and discussions,
so also it is true that when we welcome Christ, it is really
God whom we are welcoming. For that is what God is like.
That is even a sort of definition of God. I don't know a
better, or more Christian, definition of God than that. God
is He who enters our lives when, instead of striving to be
the first, we make ourselves the humble servants of the last.
And if Christ here makes the welcome we give to Himself
into the middle term between the welcome we give to the
little child and the welcome we give to God, claiming thus
to be the Mediator between the human and the divine, it is
because, being great in Himself, He came among us as
"One that serveth," utterly abasing Himself that we might
be exalted.

Yes, what Christ desires is to exalt us. That was His whole mission on earth. He wants to make us great. That day in the little house in Capernaum he wanted to make His disciples great. They had been discussing greatness. They had been seeking for themselves a false greatness. But He wanted to put something of real greatness into their lives, something of His own greatness, and of the greatness of God.

9

THE WHOLESOMENESS OF BELIEF

*And he said unto her, Daughter, thy faith hath made thee
whole.* ST. MARK V, 34.

*He saith unto the ruler of the synagogue, Be not afraid,
only believe.* VERSE 36.

MY SUBJECT is the wholesomeness of belief. The phrase
may at first strike us as an unfortunate one. We may protest
that the important thing about beliefs is not that they
should be wholesome but that they should be true. Such
a protest, however, rests largely upon a misunderstanding.
Let me then begin by trying to say first what is here meant
by belief, and then what is meant by wholesomeness.

The two English words "belief" and "faith" translate the
same word in the Greek of the New Testament, and it is
a word that is never used in the plural. Christian faith does
not mean believing a number of things, few or many: it
means a single indivisible disposition of mind and heart. It
does not mean accepting a creed: it means trusting in God.
Our Lord's complaint was not that men did not have a
creed or even that they had a wrong one. I do not suppose
He ever met a man who would have boggled at saying, "I
believe in God, the Father Almighty, Maker of heaven and
earth." Certainly the ruler of the synagogue to whom Jesus
said, "Be not afraid, only believe" would have had no difficulty in making this confession. No, Jesus' complaint was

that men seemed to lean so little upon the God of whose
reality and power they professed to have no doubt. They
put so little trust in Him when confronted with the actual
vicissitudes of life. And so they were perpetually haunted
by fear. I remember once hearing John Macmurray say,
"All through the New Testament the opposite of faith is
fear."

And now what does wholesomeness mean? What did
Jesus mean by saying, "Thy faith hath made thee whole"?
The phrase would just as well be translated, "Thy faith
hath saved thee," for the verb used is the regular New
Testament word for "save." Our two concepts of health
and salvation represent one concept in the New Testament,
and the same is true in the German language, where *Heil*
means both health and salvation. We have erroneously come
to think of salvation as having to do only or primarily with
a state of blessedness into which men may or may not pass
after they die, but how wrong this idea is may be seen from
the fact that the Old Testament writers had no notion of
a state of blessedness after death and yet are all the time
speaking about salvation.

Let us keep it in mind, then, that salvation means neither
more nor less than wholesomeness or health, which are of
course two forms of the same Anglo-Saxon word. And if it
be objected that healing has to do with the body and salvation with the soul, we must further remind ourselves that
the Bible does not work with that hard-and-fast distinction
between body and soul which we have inherited from Greek
philosophy, but which contemporary philosophy and psychology are now teaching us to correct. Nothing could be
further from the thought of the Biblical writers than the
conception of a man as "a ghost in a machine," against
which Professor Ryle of Oxford University has so vigorously
protested; for to them also man is a single and indivisible

psycho-somatic organism. We have for long been accustomed to think of the healing of the body and the salvation of the soul as two quite unrelated things; but how
wrong we were may be suspected, not only from the fact
that "heal" and "save" were the same word in our Lord's
language, but even more significantly from the fact that He
appears to have spent as much time in healing bodily diseases as in healing the diseases of the soul. Once indeed I
heard a man complain that the Four Gospels had more of
the atmosphere of the hospital about them than that of the
meeting-house! And not only so, but the two seemed to be
most closely inter-connected in our Lord's mind, as when
John the Baptist sent two of his disciples to ask Jesus
whether He were indeed the Messiah and Jesus answered,
"Go and tell John the things you hear and see; how the
blind receive their sight, the lame walk, the lepers are
cleansed, the dead are raised up, and the poor have the
Good News preached to them."

I suppose the truth is that most, if not all, of the ills that
flesh is heir to have both a somatic and a psychical side to
them, and that some approach to the healing of them may
be made from either side. One often wonders, in reading
the lives of the saints of bygone generations, whether the
periods of depression, the black humours, the darknesses and
doubts, to which they were so often subject, were not in
part due to physical causes; while on the other hand the
medical profession is every day laying greater stress on the
mental or spiritual causes of physical ailments. However
that may be, it is clear that our Lord's own approach to the
healing of all diseases was from the spiritual side. Trust in
God was His sovereign remedy. I once heard a great New
Testament scholar say that the key-word of Jesus' whole
teaching was, "All things are possible to him who believes."
It was to a woman who, as we are told, "had suffered many

things of many physicians, and had spent all that she had, and was nothing bettered but rather grew worse," that He spoke this word, "Daughter, thy faith hath healed (or saved) thee; go in peace." But He said just the same to the woman who washed His feet and dried them with her hair and anointed them with precious ointment. The one was suffering from a physical ailment—a haemorrhage; the other, we are told, was a sinner; but to each He spoke exactly the same words, "Thy faith hath saved thee; go in peace."

Do you and I enjoy this peace, this haleness and this salvation? And if we do not, what is it that stands in our way? The Bible answers with one voice, *What stands in our way is that, instead of trusting in God, we trust in ourselves.* The Bible word for trusting in ourselves is sin; for sin is simply self-centredness, no more and no less. What is wrong with mankind is that it is introverted towards itself instead of being extroverted towards God, that instead of leaning upon God it leans upon its own resources. How constantly that is said in the Old Testament, as in the hundred-and-eighteenth psalm, "It is better to trust in the Lord than to put confidence in man"; or in the Book of Proverbs, "The fear of man bringeth a snare: but whoso putteth his trust in the Lord shall be safe"; or by Jeremiah, "The way of man is not in himself: it is not in man that walketh to direct his steps." In more than one of his writings Martin Luther says that our human trouble began when mankind became *incurvatus in se*—"bent inwards towards itself," and this is something that our contemporary psychiatrists are constantly saying in their own different way. I remember hearing a distinguished contemporary of my own exclaim that even the worship of the sun would be a much more wholesome thing than mankind's worship of himself. He was speaking of the so-called Religion of Humanity as championed by Auguste Comte and his followers. To Comte,

Humanity, not God, was *le grand Être*, and it is very significant that his last words, spoken on his death-bed, were *Quelle perte irréparable!*—"What an irreparable loss!"—than which surely no statement could be more unchristian.

It is in this way that we are to understand the great New Testament conception of salvation by faith—which is the same as to say the wholesomeness of belief. "By grace are ye saved through faith," writes St. Paul. The conception has often been crudely interpreted to mean that only if our theology is orthodox during this present life can we hope to reach heaven after we die; but what it really means is that only if by the grace of God we are enabled to entrust our lives to Him can we attain, either here or hereafter, to wholeness of life, to spiritual health, to joy and peace, and to deliverance from all the fears that otherwise beset us. The service rendered by doctrinal theology is to keep our trust in God free from the many aberrations to which it is at all times subject. The New Testament frequently speaks of "sound doctrine," but I think it significant that in the Greek the phrase is *hygiainousa didaskalia*, literally "hygienic teaching." It would sound very modern if I were to say that reliance upon God rather than upon ourselves is the secret of spiritual hygiene, but actually it is not modern at all—it is in the New Testament!

I cannot think that any of us will want to deny that humanity stands in need of salvation. Something is radically wrong with us. Something is wrong with our society. The world is in a sorry muddle, making us afraid to open our newspapers every single morning, lest we read that the muddle has become still more muddled while we slept. Not all the lessons of their long history have yet taught men how to live with one another. But clearly what is wrong with our society derives from what is wrong with our individual selves. At least one phrase in the General Confession we can

all make our own: "There is no health in us." We are full
of fears, full of anxieties, full of discontents and inward
dispeace. Nor can it, I think, reasonably be doubted that
it is from a single malady we are suffering. The symptoms
are many, but they are symptoms of the same fundamental
disease. How is this disease to be diagnosed? Well, for myself I can only say that the longer I live, the more convinced
I am that the New Testament diagnosis is the true one.
It is that each of us is *incurvatus in se*. We are self-centred
both in the sense that we think too much about ourselves
and in the sense that we think too highly of our own importance in the scheme of things. I know I do both, but
I do not know it as I ought. My friends and acquaintances
are probably far more aware of my self-importance and
self-indulgence than I am myself.

How then is this deep-seated malady of mine to be
healed? I can only answer with Jeremiah and St. Paul,
"He that glorieth, let him glory in the Lord." No doubt a
partial answer would be to say that we should think less
about ourselves and more about our fellow men; for our
fellow men are the Lord's proxy—"Inasmuch as ye have
done it unto the least of these my brethren, ye have done
it unto me." Yet I must not allow this to mean that I give
the glory to the human race, vesting all my hope and all my
trust in human achievement; for St. Paul says again, "That
no flesh should glory in his presence," and "Let no man
glory in men, for . . . ye are Christ's, and Christ is God's."
It is only when I see all human achievement as dependent
upon divine grace, and my service of men to be a service
of God, that my hurt can be healed.

Such then is my conviction. Only by faith in God, only
by reposing my trust in Him, only by giving Him the sole
glory, can we be made whole. To believe that our times are
in His hand is to find a new and better way of suffering the

slings and arrows of outrageous fortune: a way of facing disappointment and defeat, accident and bereavement, sickness and the fear of death and the daily anxieties that fall to the lot of us all; but a way also of taking our successes, our little triumphs, and our joys. I like to think of the Christian religion as a frame of reference within which every one of life's exigencies is put in its true setting and given its rightful place. If we have no such faith to support us, if we are thrown back upon the strength of our own arm and the brightness of our own wits, making us take pride in human achievement and bluffing ourselves into a stoical indifference to human defeat, the whole conduct of our lives will turn sour and savourless.

And now only one last word. Perhaps somebody will say that he cannot attain to this faith. Well, I will say only this: perhaps one reason why we fail to have faith is that we do not really want it. The finding of the cure must await the diagnosis of the disease. Do we really know how ill we are? And do we know what is wrong with us? If we do not, we shall be both listless and misguided in our search for the cure. How can I find God?, we ask. I would venture to answer that God is He who is found by those who know that they themselves are lost. God is the name for the reality that breaks in upon our consciousness when we have surrendered our pride. Jesus said, "Everyone that asketh receiveth: and he that seeketh findeth: and to him that knocketh it shall be opened." And Pascal, you remember, was bold enough to make Christ say to the doubter that in the seeking itself there was a measure of finding: "Thou wouldst not be seeking me, if thou hadst not already found me: therefore disquiet not thyself." Yet let our prayer be for a fuller finding than this, a finding of greater things in God than we had ever sought or desired; remembering the familiar words of St. Bernard's hymn:

Quam bonus te quaerentibus,
Sed quid invenientibus?

How good to those who seek,
But what to those who find?

10

RELIGION AND REALITY

Behold, thou desirest truth in the inward parts.
PSALM LI, 6.

THAT is what God desires of us all—"truth in the inward parts." It is what He desires of us before and above everything else. Indeed it might be said that it is the only thing He asks of us directly. If only we are *true*, everything else that He desires of us will take care of itself, or rather He will take care of it.

But alas! how little truth there seems to be in the inward parts of most of us! Our lives are full of make-believe. Not only do we pretend to others but we are constantly pretending to ourselves; and to pretend to ourselves is of course at the same time to pretend to God. It is only to a very careful self-examination that the full extent of this pretence is likely to disclose itself. In such self-examination the greatest saints were very expert, so that nowhere will you find it carried out with more scrupulous diligence than in the pages of St. Augustine or Thomas à Kempis or John Bunyan. Such men knew their own hearts and knew how much untruth their hearts contained. And in our own scientific age a certain addition has been made to this knowledge from quite a different point of view—from the psychological and medical point of view—by Freud and his fellow psychoanalysts—so that priest and medicine man seem once again to be joining hands, as in the ancient days of our race. The psycho-analysts have revealed to our astonished and disgusted generation a hitherto unsuspected depth of deceitfulness in the hearts of us all. They have shown us how much we are at pains to evade and cover up the truth, and how little we are at pains to discover it clearly and face it honestly. They have shown us how seldom our thinking is real thinking and how much of it is in the nature of what they call an escape-mechanism or defence-mechanism. They have shown us how many of our supposed reasonings are not reasonings at all but mere rationalisations of our own prejudices and desires.

But even without such expert guidance we cannot help realising how little truth and reality there are in our lives. Listen to the talk in any drawing-room or club or railway carriage, and ask yourself how much of it is the honest reflection of honest thought. I remember once walking for a whole mile with a man who was explaining to me in the most elaborate way the reasons why he had not been appointed to a certain post. I remember how difficult I found it to give my attention to what he was saying, because I felt it was all so unreal. None of the reasons he gave had anything whatever to do with the realities of the case. He never mentioned the real reason why he had not been appointed. I knew the real reason. Everybody knew it. And I felt sure that somewhere deep down within him he knew it himself, though he was not prepared to face the shock to his self-esteem which would have been involved in its direct contemplation. And have you never caught *yourself* in the middle of some eloquent explanation which you were making to yourself or to another, and pulled yourself up sharply, because you suddenly realised that all you were saying was in the nature of an evasion?

Another very common kind of unreality in our thinking

is when, instead of caring about nothing but the truth and facing it however unexpected and unwelcome it may be, we are merely arguing with ourselves or others in defence of some received notion, some favourite idea of our own, or it may be some opinion or generalisation to which we have committed ourselves publicly in some way and which we are very loath to revise. I know in my own case, for example, what a temptation besets me to stand through thick and thin by certain opinions with which I have identified myself in my published books, and how I sometimes become aware that this little piece of personal pride is coming between my thought and the reality of which I am thinking. After all, how seldom we succeed in laying our minds right up against reality! It is only in that bare contact that truth can ever be discovered, and yet how seldom the contact is achieved! Try to imagine what an upheaval it would mean in the life you are now living, if everything false, everything faked, everything merely pretentious, were swept clean out of your life and thought, and you started to build up your whole existence again, and your whole philosophy, and also your whole reputation, on a basis of stark reality and perfect truth!

Yet this, as our text says, is exactly what God requires of us. And, in a sense, it is all He requires of us. God Himself *is* the Truth. He *is* the ultimate Reality. And therefore He knows that He can find no entrance into any soul, nor any soul find access to Him, except in that contact of the naked mind with naked reality in which alone truth can be apprehended. In that contact is God's only opportunity and He is more than ready to take all the risks of it. He says to us, as it were, "Be honest with yourself, be straight in your thinking, get down in the foundations of your life to bare reality—and leave the rest to Me." *What* we find when, having brushed aside all the unrealities, we get down to the bare reality of life—that is not our concern, but God's alone.

Now when true religion comes into a man's life, this is exactly what happens to him—he faces the reality of life for the first time. To be converted is simply to come to honest terms with oneself and with God. We have been living falsely, we have been dodging the issue, we have been evading our most solemn responsibilities, we have been avoiding too realistic a scrutiny of our working ideals and motives; and then, perhaps quite suddenly, there comes over us an overwhelming wave of realisation, and we see ourselves as we are, and life as it is, and God as He is. Or again you may observe a boy awakening, perhaps in the period of his adolescence, to the solemn meaning of life. He may have been a fine young fellow all along, but now somehow his life becomes readjusted and reorganised on a deeper level. He was never indeed what men would call a liar, but he sees now how far he nevertheless was from being "steel-true and blade-straight." He understands now what is meant by "truth in the inward parts." Such is the wonderful and beautiful thing that so often, by the grace of God, happens to our lads and lasses in association with their first communion; and it is by far the most wonderful and beautiful thing that can be observed in the whole range of our human life.

I have said that Freud and his *confrères* have done us a real service in enabling us to realise from a somewhat different point of view the depth of untruth and unreality that there is in the lives of us all, until some such radical readjustment is effected. And yet Freud himself completely misunderstands the office of true religion in regard to this readjustment. By him, as by so many others among our contemporaries, religion is regarded, not as an honest facing of reality, but as an escape from it. It is, they say, part of our defence against the truth rather than part of our acceptance of it. And God, they say, instead of being the Reality we find when we make an end of all evasion, is only a projection of our own desires and prejudices—or, in another phrase, "a subjectively generated illusion." Now undoubtedly there is a true sense in which religion is an escape and God is a Refuge. Religion is an escape from the fuss and fret and pettiness of our merely material interests to the serenity and largeness of the things of the spirit. But to those who have learned that the things of the spirit are more real than the things of the body and of earth, it can never seem an escape from *reality*. I do not doubt, indeed, that the formulas and rituals of religion are constantly used as an escape, and as an evasion of that very reality which they are intended to make us face. The altar has often been used as a hiding-place from God rather than as a place of meeting with Him face to face. This is what Iago in *Othello* calls "Divinity of Hell":—

> Divinity of hell!
> When devils will their blackest sins put on,
> They do suggest at first with heavenly shows.

That is false religion; and I fear we should have to admit that there is much more of it in the world than there is of true religion. But anyone who has ever been visited by the authentic experiences of which I have spoken, or who has even observed them in others, must know beyond all cavil that a conversion to true religion means a conversion away from all evasion to "truth in the inward parts."

But what now of those among us who, when they have done all that in them lies to purge their minds and hearts of unreality and have sought the truth long and carefully and with tears, have nevertheless not seemed to find God? I number men among my own acquaintances who seem to me to have been marvellously honest in their quest and who

yet complain that when they have got down as near to reality as they were able, it was not God they found. Well,
there is much one might say about such troubled spirits,
but I am concerned now to say only one thing, namely this:
Let such see to it that they are absolutely honest in their
quest, and then *what they find* is not their responsibility
but His whom they seek. God is willing to take all the risks
of honest enquiry. If in your search for truth you have not
found God, do not stop seeking but look deeper. Do not
stop thinking, but think more truly. Make sure that there is
nothing in your heart that is warping the straightness of your
thought. Make sure that it is nothing in *you* that is keeping
God out—preventing you from seeing His glory and hearing His call to service.

Real harm has, I believe, been done to the cause of religion by those voices of our time which, alarmed by the
number of those who have seemed to seek God without
finding Him, have counselled the despair of thought rather
than its deeper exercise and a retreat from the quest rather
than a yet more eager pursuit of it. Such counsellors have
provided too much semblance of excuse for the schoolboy's
definition of faith as "believing what you know ain't true."
But true religion has nothing to fear, but rather everything
to gain, from honesty and courageous thinking and plain
speaking. If God is Truth and Truth is God, it is not by
probing less deeply that we are likely to reach Him but by
probing more deeply than we have ever probed before.
There is indeed a kind of abstract thinking that may lead
us sadly astray from Him, the kind of thinking in which
"the native hue of resolution is sicklied o'er by the pale
cast of thought"; but such thinking is not real thinking and
it is not deep thinking. And for myself it becomes daily
clearer to me that if ever I have seemed to fail to find God
—the God who was all the time seeking me—it was not be-

cause I had thought too well, but because I had not thought well enough, because there was too little reality in my thinking and too little truth in my life.

What God desires of us all is truth. But that does not mean that His *primary* desire is that we should accept a creed. Some men say, "Religion consists in the docile and unintelligent acceptance of a mass of antiquated doctrines"; and having said that, they suppose themselves justified in leaving religion severely alone. But to say anything like that to oneself is to be guilty of a serious evasion. God's primary demand is only that we should ourselves be true and leave the rest to Him. Forcing oneself to believe things is no part of true religion. It is Truth itself that must do the forcing. Faith is a gift of God, and He alone can give it to us; we cannot give it to ourselves. "I am the Way," our Lord says, "and the Truth, and the Life." Let us not deceive ourselves by saying that Christ wants us to give up the search for Truth and accept Him instead. It is only as the Truth that He wants to be accepted. He is confident, and His Church is confident, that the more honest men are with themselves, the more likely they are to find Him and be found of Him. Make no mistake about it: the demand that God is making upon you now is a demand for "truth in the inward parts."

11

A UNIVERSITY SERMON

Behold, I send you forth as sheep in the midst of wolves:
be ye therefore wise as serpents, and harmless as doves.
ST. MATTHEW X, 16.

THIS was Christ's injunction to His twelve disciples when
He first sent them out into the world. It must therefore be
accepted as a definition of the authentic and original Christian temper, and as a mirror for saints.

If we took them separately, the two halves of the injunction would yield two very different conceptions of the
Christian temper, and it may be that some of us will prefer
one and some the other. Not long ago I was surprised to
hear a friend of mine, who is a true lover of the Gospel,
exclaim that he wished Christ had never said the bit about
being wise as serpents. On the other hand I remember hearing a German theologian remark in my student days that
Christianity had suffered badly through too much being
made of such talk about doves and about sheep, and that
our Lord's own reputation had suffered through the application to Him of the Old Testament saying, "He is
brought as a lamb to the slaughter, and as a sheep before
her shearers is dumb, so he openeth not his mouth."

Well, I do not agree with either of these opinions, and
what I am going to argue is that both halves of our Lord's
injunction are equally valid, and equally necessary to an

understanding of the true pattern of Christian saintliness.

Take first "harmless as doves"—though I think "harmless" is not quite the right English word—"guileless" would be better. Nothing, surely, stands out more clearly in the evangelists' portrait of the Lord Himself than His utter guilelessness. His was a simplicity of character, a transparency of motive, a frankness of approach such as cannot elsewhere be matched. The attempted representations of Christ in art and literature are many and varied, but I think this simplicity and lack of guile is a common feature of them all. And we have not only this particular injunction, but also much else in His teaching, to show that He demanded the like of His followers. If He said only once that they were to be as doves, He said many times that they were to be as little children. "Unless you turn back, and become as little children, you shall not enter into the kingdom of heaven." The word translated "turn back" is significant. It implies that as we grow up to maturity, we inevitably lose the simplicity of childhood, and develop increasingly intricate natures. We become shrewd and crafty and deep. We have come to know our world, and the complexities of the world are reflected in the defences we raise against it. Therefore, said Christ, we must "turn back."

But He said also, "Be ye wise as serpents." The simile, I grant you, is a little startling, but it was familiar to His hearers from the Old Testament saying that "the serpent was more subtle than any beast of the field which the Lord God had made." It is clear, then, that in turning back to be as little children, we are not to divest ourselves of the characteristic gains of maturity. Our Lord's own wisdom is no less stressed in the records than His simplicity. St. Luke tells us that as He grew older, "He increased in wisdom and stature, and in favour with God and man," and it would seem that not until His thirtieth year did He find Himself sufficiently mature to enter upon His public career. But every phase of that career then bears on it the mark of full maturity. Jesus Christ knew His world. He knew what was in man. He understood the human situation and cherished no illusions about it. Little children are often happily ignorant of the harsher facts of life, and care sits lightly on them; but this is He who was called the Man of Sorrows, who took upon Himself the whole burden of the world's evil and the world's pain, and was Himself, as we are told, made perfect through the things which He suffered. If to be wise means to have looked into life's most tragic depths and come to terms with all one saw there, then where was ever a wisdom like the wisdom of Jesus Christ? The evangelists tell us how again and again He would be heckled by His learned opponents, the Scribes and Pharisees. They would think up the kind of questions we call "posers" and put them to Him. But His answer was always such that, as the evangelists say in more than one context, "no man durst ask Him any more questions." His disciples cannot have been in any doubt what He meant when He spoke of a mature wisdom that went hand in hand with a guileless simplicity.

We think we understand it too. We know that guilelessness does not mean gullibility. We know that there is a simplicity which is not that of a simpleton. And above all we think we understand the difference between child*like*-ness and child*ish*ness. Yes, but do we always realise that we would not have understood any of these things apart from Christ? Do we realise that the existence in our language of that distinction between childlikeness and childishness derives entirely from His teaching? He was the first to find in childhood something that was not childish, just as He was the first to discover a humility that was not less but more noble than pride, and a meekness that was not cringing and abject. This conjunction of wisdom and simplicity is therefore peculiarly His own, and provides the unique and specific pattern of Christian saintliness.

It is, I think, St. Paul who has given us the best formula for the understanding of this conjunction. "Brethren," he wrote to the Corinthian Christians, "be not children in understanding: howbeit in malice ['evil' would be a better translation] be ye children, but in understanding be men." The melancholy fact is that as we leave the simplicities of childhood behind us, we grow at the same time in understanding and in evil. Every expansion of our knowledge is sooner or later used by us for the furtherance of our own selfish ends. Understanding is therefore not a good thing in itself and by itself, as the ages of rationalism fondly thought. The serpent too was wise and subtle. The devils also believe and tremble. Understanding is a good thing only when conjoined to guilelessness. Knowledge, we say, is power; but it is power for evil no less than for good. And as I look back over my own growth, I can plainly see how each new step forward in my understanding of the nature of things, of my own body and my own mental powers, and of the world of men about me, provided me with an additional opportunity of arranging things to my own fleshly and worldly advantage. The measure of our understanding is indeed the measure of our maturity. It is only by getting to know our world that we can grow up at all; but the tragedy is that none of us actually does succeed in thus getting to know our world without allowing ourselves to get caught in its toils and so becoming what the Bible calls worldly-minded.

I believe we all know in our inmost hearts that we lost something very precious as we grew from childhood to full maturity, and I am quite sure that we owe this realisation to the influence of Jesus Christ. We know that what we ought to have done was to use our advancing knowledge and understanding in the service of a still inviolate simplicity and guilelessness, and at the same time we know that we actually did use it in very large part for their destruction. Therefore there is nothing for it but to "turn back and become as little children" again. Not that we are to divest ourselves of any part of the knowledge and understanding we have acquired. That would be in one sense impossible and in another sense entirely wrong—a betrayal of the talents with which we have been entrusted. Rather must our search for knowledge continue as eagerly as ever. "When I was a child," St. Paul writes, ". . . . I understood as a child; but when I became a man, I put away childish things." And he has no intention at all of going back on that. "Be *not* children in understanding," he says; only "in evil be ye children." That, I am sure, is the true pattern of Christian saintliness, and the true guide to the Christian conduct of life—to learn all we can, and acquire all the skill we can, yet to remain quite simple, single-hearted, utterly without guile, "wise as serpents, and harmless as doves."

It is our guide to the conduct of all life, but I have chosen to speak of it today because I believe it is in a special sense our guide to the conduct of university life. The purpose of education is to make us wise; and the education now available to us in our universities is so exhaustive, not to say exhausting, that those of us who have submitted ourselves to it certainly ought to be "wise as serpents." Just think how tiny was the sum of available knowledge in Palestine in our Lord's day compared with what is offered in the University of Edinburgh. What did our Lord's contemporaries know of geography, of geology, of biology, of physics, of chemistry, of astronomy, compared with what even the first-year student is taught today? And what did they know of human history and pre-history, of psychology, of economics, of logic and philosophy? In our Lord's time the sum of available knowledge was so small that a diligent student could aspire to master the whole of it within a few years. Even in the famous schools of Greece, where scientific knowledge was immensely greater than among the Jews, students did not need to specialise; they were just taught everything there was to know. But now the sum of knowledge is so great that each student has to make a very small selection from among the various branches of knowledge, and even then he can be given only the elements in these few branches. If he wants to attain anything like mastery he must specialise further and, in fact, choose a single branch; or rather he must choose, not a whole branch, but something much more like a twig! Not only must the chemist abandon hope of being expert in anything but chemistry, but he cannot possibly be expert in the whole of chemistry; nor the historian in the whole of history.

I suppose what most of us try to do is to take in as much as our minds can hold. We learn a little about a great many things, and then a little more about a few things—"learning more and more about less and less." It's a bit of a scramble, no doubt, and we are always trying to catch up. Nevertheless most of us who have enjoyed such a modern education are inclined to be very conscious of our intellectual superiority over our unlettered neighbours. The modern intellectual, with his understanding of the constitution of the physical universe, his outlook on world history, or his insight into the psychological and physiological constitution of human nature, is very apt to imagine himself as sitting in the royal box, surveying from this special point of vantage the human scene below. These others still speak as children, they think as children, they understand as children; but himself—he is become a man and has put away childish things.

What, then, does our Lord mean when He says to *us*, as He certainly does say to us, that we are to turn back and become as little children again? I know. I know from my own case. And I think we all know. We know that, however great has been our gain in acquiring all this elaborate intellectual equipment, we have also all the time been in mortal danger of losing something—of losing the most precious thing of all, without which all that we have gained is just so much useless lumber and rubble. We have been in danger of losing our simplicity, our guilelessness, our singleness of heart and our singleness of purpose; and to lose these things, says Christ, is to lose the Kingdom.

I think this danger is twofold. It arises in a special way from the great variety and complexity of modern knowledge. Our learning comes to us in bits and pieces. We learn something of this subject and something of that; and we are seldom very clear how the different so-called subjects fit into one another; and still less are we clear what relation they bear to the solemn purpose of life as a whole. So often we students are like Martha in the Gospel; we are careful and troubled about many things to the neglect of the one thing needful. The complexity of our interests has never been resolved into a unity, and this unresolved complexity is reflected in our inmost souls, which grow turbid and confused, losing even such transparency and simplicity as they once possessed. That for one thing; but there is also the danger of intellectual pride, a danger which none of us escapes. We think that knowledge is worth having for its own sake alone, and as such confers a certain dignity on its possessor. That, however, is the fondest of illusions. In a recently published book I read the sentence: "Although the average cultivated person *knows* a great deal, what he *is* is something relatively insignificant." It is quite certainly true that "though I . . . understand all mysteries and all knowledge . . . and have not love, it profiteth me nothing" at all.

Don't we all know in our hearts that the fundamental human problem is exactly the same for us who are variously learned as for the most illiterate of our contemporaries? I suppose that is what Mr. Aldous Huxley means when he writes that "the course of every intellectual, if he pursues his journey long and unflinchingly enough, ends in the obvious, from which the non-intellectuals have never stirred." Only one thing is needful; and it is the same thing for them and for us; and we all know what it is. It is so easy to pretend that our learning has made a difference, that for us the ultimate issue is no longer quite so simple. It is so easy to find in our studies an escape from the plain alternative of plain obedience or disobedience to the commandments of God—from the plain alternative of accepting Christ or rejecting Him—from the plain alternative of being born only after the flesh or being born again of the Spirit. But don't we all know in our hearts that when we think such thoughts, we are cheating? I believe there is no more wholesome discipline for university folk than to cultivate the acquaintance, or to read the biographies of the simplest of Christ's saints. I have myself recently been reading the biographies of two young women whom the Roman Church has lately canonized; that of St. Marie Bernarde of Lourdes, who was the dunce of an elementary school in the South of France; and that of St. Theresa of Lisieux, who, though quicker-witted and better-instructed than the other, knew hardly more of what is taught and learned in universities. We do not canonize people in our Protestant Churches, but that is not for lack of many saintly souls of an equally guileless simplicity.

Now, needless to say, I do not at all envy these simple saints for their lack of intellectual equipment. I am profoundly grateful for the larger opportunities of learning which I have myself enjoyed; at least I hope I am grateful, and not merely *proud*. I have no intention of surrendering any of the knowledge I have acquired, and I intend to go on learning and studying and researching as long as life lasts. Yet I should a thousand times rather that we were all as they than that we should end up as cynical and disillusioned intellectuals, or as dry-as-dust scholars, or as soulless pedants wise only in their own conceit, or as walking encyclopaedias useful only for recondite reference, or as starchy blue-stockings, or as any of the other insufferable types which are far too often seen in our university common rooms, both junior and senior, and which far too often emerge from our universities to cumber the good ground outside! You and I have been given the chance of acquiring a degree of knowledge, and a kind of wisdom and subtlety which is denied to a majority of our fellows. For that great privilege let us give due thanks to God. But what Christ is saying to us in this word which I have tried to expound is that all our knowledge, all our wisdom and all our subtlety, will at best be mere froth and bubble, and at worst will bring our immortal souls to final destruction unless, by bringing them into the service of a childlike simplicity and a plain obedience, we remain at the same time as harmless and guileless as doves.

12

MAN'S DOMINION OVER NATURE

For it was not to angels that God subjected the world to come, of which we are speaking. It has been testified somewhere, "What is man that thou are mindful of him, or the son of man, that thou carest for him? Thou didst make him a little lower than the angels, thou hast crowned him with glory and honour, putting everything in subjection under his feet." Now in putting everything in subjection to man, he left nothing outside his control. As it is, we do not yet see everything in subjection to him. But we see Jesus, who for a little while was made lower than the angels, crowned with glory and honour because of the suffering of death, so that by the grace of God he might taste death for every man.

HEBREWS II, 5–9. R.S.V. *(except for the last word)*.

I WANT to offer you as faithful an exposition of that passage as I can, taking it clause by clause.

Man's dominion over nature is one of the very first things to be affirmed in Holy Scripture. It is in the first chapter of Genesis. "Then God said, Let us make man in our image, after our likeness: and let them have dominion over the fish of the sea, and over the fowl of the air, and over the cattle, and over all the earth, and over every creeping thing that creepeth upon the earth." The only way God *could* have given man this power was by making him in His own image, by endowing him with some measure of what He Himself possessed in perfection, namely, intelligence, self-knowledge and the ability to "look before and after." As John Calvin explains in expounding the Genesis passage, "The image of God extends to everything in which the nature of man surpasses that of all other species of animals." In creating him thus and giving him this universal dominion, God "crowned him with glory and honour," as is here quoted from the eighth psalm. The Bible, therefore, does not allow us to think meanly of the human race. The dignity of man is a fundamental Christian doctrine. You and I are dignitaries in God's universe, wearing crowns of glory and honour. "What a piece of work is man!" Hamlet exclaimed; and that is not surprising, if he is not only God's work but a work made in God's own image, a kind of copy of Himself.

1. This is a dignity out of which we cannot contract. You and I cannot change our status in God's universe, nor can we shed the least part of the responsibilities which that status entails. It would often be so convenient if we could do this. I find that when I want to do something low or mean, or even dubious, the first thing I have to do, in order to get away with it, is to suppress the knowledge that I am made in God's image. If I am tempted to lustful action, I cannot give myself the green light to go ahead, until or unless I tell myself that it does not matter all that much what an ordinary fellow like me does, that I am only one among spawning billions of living creatures to whom such action is quite natural, that I like them am merely part of nature—or something else of that kind. Yet I cannot say that I've ever had much comfort from the pretence. This same epistle speaks of how Moses, with the fleshpots of Egypt before him, was tempted to enjoy "the pleasures of sin for a season." But the pleasures of sin are spoiled for us, as they would have been spoiled for Moses had he yielded to them, by the secret knowledge that we are all

the time crowned with glory and honour. There are some things which you just can't comfortably do with a crown on your head—especially a crown that won't come off, however much you disgrace it and defile it! I remember a memorable day when I heard a king say in a broadcast, "I renounce the throne." But we can't do that. Our royal station in God's universe is something that we cannot resign.

And that means that we cannot contract out of our dominion over nature, or out of the many responsible decisions with which that dominion confronts us every day of our lives. We are all aware that our power over nature has been immensely increased in recent times by the advance of modern science. We now have the power to blow up every living thing—I was going to say "to atoms"; but it's more than that, it is to blow up the very atoms of which they are composed; and soon—who knows?—we may have the power to blow up the old planet itself. The responsibility thus created is so terrifying that we are frequently tempted to call a halt to the advance of science, placing a ban on further scientific research. Yet in doing so, we should not really be contracting out of our responsibility, but rather taking what is itself a most responsible decision, and I believe a very wrong and unworthy one. God meant us to discover all we can about nature, and to gain as much control over it as we can, or He would not have endowed us with the intelligence we have. "He left nothing outside man's control," says our text. It was in His mercy that He did this; for think of all that advancing science has enabled us to do for the relief of human suffering, in healing the sick, in feeding the hungry, in clothing the naked. To put the slightest brake on scientific thought might be as fatal to the continuance of the race as the wrong application of it of which we are now living in fear; for it might prevent developments of medicine, agriculture and engineering which may very well prove necessary to that continuance. I will hear no word against science, or against its unlimited advancement. Its triumphs are among the brightest jewels in man's crown of glory and honour, or would be if only he did not drag them in the mud of his own hatreds and jealousies and greeds, instead of using them in the service of his fellows and for the greater glory of God.

II. Our text goes on to say that though God left nothing out of man's control, yet "as things are, we do not yet see everything in subjection to him." In spite of all the power that modern science has placed in our hands, we know that to be only too true. Indeed it may even strike us as a ridiculous understatement. As things are, we hardly know whether to be more impressed by man's power or by his impotence. Pascal, you remember, spoke in a single celebrated phrase of "the grandeur and misery of man," not knowing on which to lay the greater stress. And so also Alexander Pope, when in his famous *Essay on Man* he called him "the glory, jest and riddle of the world." Pope like Pascal was writing at a time when the first great triumphs of modern experimental science were just beginning to be digested by the public mind, and here are the lines next following in his verse:

The glory, jest and riddle of the world.

Go, wondrous creature! mount where Science guides;
    Go, measure earth, weigh air, and state the tides;
    Instruct the planets in what orbs to run,
    Correct old Time, and regulate the Sun . . .
    Go, teach Eternal Wisdom how to rule—
    Then drop into thyself, and be a fool!

Listen also to what an Elizabethan poet, Sir John Davies, had written a hundred and fifty years earlier:

I know my soul hath power to know all things,
Yet is she blind and ignorant in all:
I know I'm one of Nature's little kings,
Yet to the least and vilest things am thrall.

I know my life's a pain and but a span;
I know my sense is mock'd in everything;
And, to conclude, I know myself a Man—
Which is a proud and yet a wretched thing.

III. Well, the writer of this New Testament epistle is aware of the same anomaly when he says that though God put everything in subjection to man and left nothing outside his control, nevertheless we do not yet see everything in subjection to him. What then is it that limits our dominion? Why is there still at least as much misery as there is of grandeur in the life of mankind? We should have to reply, shouldn't we, that there are two reasons? The first is that our control of nature, remarkable as it is and even more remarkable as it may one day become, comes up after all against certain fixed limits which it cannot pass. We must all die. Science may enable us to prolong our lives a little, but there seems no hope of science destroying this last enemy, as St. Paul called it. Not long ago I met on the street a University colleague of mine who had been rather ill, and I asked him how he did. "I'm a bit better," he replied, "but of course we are all fighting a losing battle." And it is only too true. Death will get us all in the end. That, then, we would say, is the first reason, but the second is that through our folly and wickedness we woefully misuse even the powers we have, constantly turning into a curse what was given us as a blessing. In one of his books Reinhold Niebuhr quotes a scientist of the last generation as having said, "The superman built the aeroplane, but the ape-man seems to have got hold of it." So today we might say, "The superman released atomic energy, but the ape-man seems to have got hold of it."

We habitually think of these two—of death and sin—as two separate hindrances to our dominion, two separate causes of our distressful situation. But the writer of this epistle, and indeed the whole New Testament, thinks of them rather as very closely interconnected. They are both the work of what the New Testament writers call the same "powers of darkness." Sin and death somehow hang together. "The soul that sinneth, it shall die," writes an Old Testament prophet. "When lust hath conceived," writes St. James, "it bringeth forth sin; and sin, when it is full-grown, bringeth forth death." "The wages of sin is death," writes St. Paul, and again, "The sting of death is sin." It is by the joint operation of sin and death that human hopes are frustrated, and not until these are together conquered in the same final victory can man be made secure in his dominion, with all things under his control.

IV. But next our text goes on: "We do not yet see everything in subjection to man. But we see Jesus." That is all the writer can say to cheer us up. *We see Jesus.* Our dominion over nature is far from complete, but we see Jesus. We are all doomed to die, but we see Jesus. Such dominion as we have brings more trouble than felicity, more problems than solutions, but we see Jesus. We cannot get rid of the devils that harass us, but we see Jesus. We cannot master our sinful propensities, but we see Jesus. He means that when we look around us for some ground of hope, we see Him and nobody else. Does that perhaps seem a little naïve? Well, honestly, who or what else is there? Is there anybody or anything else to which you can really pin your hope? Do *you* see any way out except by holding on to Him? Frankly, I don't. If the influence of Jesus were ut-

terly to disappear from our society, if mankind were to un-
learn all it has learned from Him, I honestly don't know
where I could turn for the least ray of hope. As far as I can
see, it would then, as in the title of H. G. Wells's last
gloomy book, be a case of "mind at the end of its tether."
I must therefore say with Christina Rossetti:

> None other Lamb, none other Name,
> None other Hope in heaven or earth or sea,
> None other Hiding-place from guilt and shame,
>   None beside Thee.

v. But lastly our author goes on to give a reason, and it
is a reason that merits our careful consideration. "We see
Jesus, who for a little while was made lower than the angels,
crowned with glory and honour because of the suffering
of death, so that by the grace of God he might taste death
for every man." You remember he began the passage by
saying, "It was not to angels that God subjected the world
to come"—but to man. It was not to angels but to man
that He promised dominion over nature. It was not angels
but men that He crowned with glory and honour. Hence
our Saviour, whatever else He was, had to be a *Man*. Milton
was right when he spoke of "loss of Eden, Till one greater
Man restore us." An angel could not save us, but only one
who was one of ourselves, one who like ourselves was (for
a little time at least) lower than the angels, one who had
to die as we all have to die. Only because He was a man, a
mortal, as was proved by His having to suffer death, had He
the right to wear *man's* crown of glory and honour. But
because He was not only man, but at the same time God
manifest in human flesh, with all things in subjection to
Him as they are not in subjection to us, and because He
used His dominion only for the glory of the Father, whereas
the rest of us use ours for our own glory, we find in Him

the promise of all we now lack. When we see *this* Man, our hope for the human race and for each single individual within it, is wonderfully re-established. Yes, says our author, for every single individual. "He tasted death for *every* man." So to each one of us here today, Jesus says, in the words of the medieval mystery play called *Everyman,* which you will find printed in each volume in the Everyman's Library:

> Everyman, I will go with thee and be thy guide,
> In thy most need to go by thy side.

Well, I've done my best to expound this passage of scripture for you. Have I been faithful in my exposition? Don't take it from me, but read the passage again for yourself— the second chapter of the Epistle to the Hebrews, verses five to nine.

And now let me sum up in two sentences. There is only one way open to the world in the present age whereby man's understanding of, and consequent dominion over, nature can be safely exercised, and that is by making them subservient to the ends which Jesus Christ has taught us to seek. Second, there is only one way in which you individually can safely exercise your private dominion, your own God-given intellectual powers and that dangerous freedom of choice which enables you in so large a measure to control your own destiny, and that is to make it all over to Jesus Christ—to take His yoke upon you, and learn of Him, that you may find rest unto your soul. There is no other hope for the world: there is no other hope for you.

13

WHITEWASH

*Because, even because they have seduced my people, say-
ing, Peace; and there was no peace; and one built up a
wall, and, and, lo, others daubed it with untempered mortar:
say unto them which daub it with untempered mortar,
that it shall fall: there shall be an overflowing shower; and
ye, O great hailstones, shall fall; and a stormy wind shall
rend it. Lo, when the wall is fallen, shall it not be said
unto you, Where is the daubing wherewith ye have daubed
it? Therefore saith the Lord God; I will even rend it with
a stormy wind in my fury; and there shall be an overflowing shower in mine anger, and great hailstones, in my fury,
to consume it. So will I break down the wall that you have
daubed with untempered mortar, and bring it down to the
ground, so that the foundation thereof shall be discovered,
and it shall fall and ye shall be consumed in the midst
thereof: and ye shall know that I am the Lord. Thus will I
accomplish my wrath upon the wall, and upon them that
have daubed it with untempered mortar; and will say unto
you, The wall is no more, neither they that daubed it; to
wit, the prophets of Israel which prophesy concerning
Jerusalem, and which see visions of peace for her, and
there is no peace, saith the Lord God.*

EZEKIEL XIII, 10–16.

THIS is a good and typical example of Hebrew prophecy,
so I shall begin by putting the question, What is a prophet?
We are so apt to answer that he is a man who can foresee
future events because he is clairvoyant and has the gift of

second sight. But I should define a prophet rather as a man of deep spiritual discernment to whom something of the will of God has been revealed, and that is something very different; because people who claim the gift of second sight are often people of very little spiritual discernment. The prophets of Israel were able to foretell future events, because God had endowed them with the power of understanding present events. They were men who discerned the signs of the times. They were men who brought the word of God to bear in so radical a way upon the life of the people that they could foresee very clearly both the judgements and the blessings for which the nation was heading.

I say "both the judgements and the blessings." All the prophets believed that the nation will ultimately be blessed by God, but the greater part of what they wrote was concerned with judgement. Whenever the Word of God is radically brought to bear upon our sinful human life, there must be much talk of judgement. In ancient Israel there were a great many false prophets as well as a few true ones, and perhaps the chief mark of the false prophet was that the note of judgement was absent from his teaching. He could see nothing wrong with the life of the people or with the way things were going in the nation. He cried peace when there was no peace. He was ready to whitewash everything. Therefore he was not really a prophet, but only pretended to be one. As this chapter begins by saying, they prophesied only "out of their own minds," and were not really declaring the Word of the Lord.

Let me read you our text again, but this time as it appears in Dr. Moffatt's modern translation:

Since they mislead my people by saying 'All is well,' when all is not well, since these daubers whitewash any flimsy wall run up to safeguard the people, tell such daubers that a deluge of rain is coming, huge hailstones shall come down, and a stormy blast shall break out, till down falls the flimsy wall; and then you will be asked, will you not, 'What about your whitewash?' The Lord the Eternal proclaims: I will let loose a stormy blast in my wrath, a deluge of rain in my anger, and hailstones in my fury, destroying the wall you daubed with your whitewash, demolishing it till its very foundations are laid bare; the wall shall fall, and crush you under it—to let you know that I am the Eternal. This will satisfy my wrath against the wall and those who daubed it with their whitewash. You will be asked, 'Where is the wall? Where are those who daubed it?—these prophets of Israel who prophesy about Jerusalem with their visions of "All is well" for her, when all is not well!' The Lord the Eternal has spoken.

It is, I say, a good example of real prophecy. The prophets of Israel, and none of them more than Jeremiah and Ezekiel, were always declaring against whitewash. In their heart of hearts the Israelites knew that their way of life left a great deal to be desired, but they were always trying to suppress this self-knowledge, and to set up in their minds what the psychologists now call "defence-mechanisms" to cover it up. They were building flimsy walls, says Ezekiel, and then whitewashing them to make them look more solid. And hosts of false prophets were all the time encouraging them to do it. Moreover, it was not only the civic life that was thus being whitewashed, but also the church life; not only the life of the court and market-place but also the life of the Temple. It is a mistake to think of the prophetic denunciations as denunciations pronounced by the Church on the world, or by religious folk upon unbelievers. Rather is it the *religion* of the people that has to bear the main brunt of their judgments. "Thus saith the Lord, . . . I hate, I despise your feast days, and I will not smell in your solemn assemblies. Though ye offer me burnt offerings and your meat offerings, I will not accept them: neither will I regard the peace offerings of your fat beasts. Take thou away from me the noise of thy songs; for I will not hear the melody of thy viols. But let judgment run down as waters, and righteousness as a mighty stream." It is thus that all true prophets have spoken. All down the ages they have exposed nothing so ruthlessly as the whitewashing of the life of the church. They have believed with St. Peter that "judgment must begin at the house of God." They have indeed been thorns in the sides of kings and parliaments, of merchants and financiers, but even more have they been thorns in the sides of churchmen, of priests and ecclesiastics, and—let me add—of General Assemblies and presbyteries and kirk sessions.

The Lord Jesus Christ was a prophet. Our forefathers spoke of the three offices of Christ, and prophecy was the first of them. Like other prophets He brought the Word of God to bear most ruthlessly upon our human life, and upon nothing more ruthlessly than the church life of His day. It was by attempting to cleanse the Temple that he courted martyrdom. His most devastating judgements were not upon "the multitude who knew not the law," not upon "the publicans and sinners," but upon the priests, the scribes, the Pharisees and the Sadducees. And there was nothing that He held against them more than their use of whitewash. "Woe unto you, scribes and Pharisees, hypocrites! for ye are like unto whited sepulchres, which indeed appear beautiful outwardly, but are within full of dead men's bones, and of all uncleanness. Even so ye also outwardly appear righteous unto men, but within ye are full of hypocrisy and iniquity." When we read that, we are inclined to say to ourselves that these churchmen of our Lord's time must have been a particularly horrible set of villains, and certainly infinitely worse than any of ourselves are ever even tempted to be. But in so thinking we are not only falsifying history but are skilfully evading the lesson which this chapter of history was intended to teach us. The Pharisees, as a matter of fact, were not at all bad people when judged by ordinary standards. But our Lord did not judge them by ordinary standards, nor does He judge us by ordinary standards. The Pharisees were the respectable pillars of the Church of their day, and the words our Lord spoke about them were meant also for us who are the pillars of the Church in our modern day. "All scripture," we are told, "is profitable for doctrine, for reproof, for correction, for instruction in righteousness," and we have not read this Scripture as we ought until we ourselves have been reproved and corrected and instructed by it.

In the early Christian Church the prophetic office was fully recognised alongside the offices of apostle and of teacher. St. Paul had written that "God hath set forth some in the Church, first apostles, secondarily prophets, thirdly teachers." St. Paul himself was an apostle, but I think he was a prophet too, and as a prophet he denounced the whitewashing of the Church. He called Ananias, the high priest of his day, "a whited wall," who judged other people according to a law he did not himself observe. As time went on, prophets ceased to be recognised as a special class, but that does not mean that they ceased to exist. From time to time there would still arise, and to our own day there have continued to arise, within the Church, men of God who have brought the Word of God to bear in the same old ruthless way upon the life both of the Church and of the world.

One such was Tertullian, the Roman lawyer and soldier's son who was converted to Christianity towards the end of the second century. Christianity was then only some five generations old, but Tertullian saw that it was already beginning to be conformed to the world, and he set him-

self with passionate vehemence to counteract that tendency.

Another such was Savonarola, the great preacher of fif-
teenth-century Florence, whose story as told in George
Eliot's *Romola* used to thrill me in my schooldays. How he
thundered from the pulpit of San Marco against the abuses
in the Church and the corrupt life of the city, ruthlessly
tearing away the veil of official complacence which covered
so much that was evil! The pope, Alexander VI, tried every
possible means of silencing him, but when he failed, took
the other line of offering him a cardinal's hat. Savonarola
replied, "No red hat will I have but that of a martyr, red-
dened with my own blood!" And martyred he was, burnt
to death in the market-place among a cheering mob.

It was less than twenty years after his death that Luther,
another great prophet, nailed his 95 theses to the door of
the church in Wittenberg—on 31st October, 1517, thereby
setting in motion the Protestant Reformation. These theses
were a terrible denunciation of the corruption of the Church,
and of the various whitewashing devices employed to cover
up that corruption. In one of them he quoted this very
text of Ezekiel. His thesis number 92 reads thus: "Away
with all those [false prophets] who say to the people of
Christ, 'Peace, peace,' when there is no peace."

Among the most remarkable of modern prophets was
Sören Kierkegaard, the Danish thinker who died just over
a hundred years ago. Never was there a more passionate
Christian than Kierkegaard, but he was a dreadfully uncomfortable thorn in the side of the nineteenth-century
Danish Church. No doubt he was an extremist, as Tertullian and Savonarola and Luther were extremists. Not all
that these prophets said was wise, and certainly not all they
said was judicious; and Kierkegaard too said much that was

not wise and judicious; but it is impossible to read him without being shaken out of our accustomed complacency. Everyone in Denmark, he says, claims to be a Christian, but how many are Christians in the New Testament sense? "The sort of men who now live," he writes, "cannot stand anything as strong as the Christianity of the New Testament (they would die of it or lose their minds), just in the same sense that children cannot stand wine, and so we prepare for them a little lemonade—and official Christianity is simply lemonade—twaddle for the sort of beings who are now called men; it is the strongest thing they can stand, and this twaddle in their language they call Christianity, just as Danish children call their lemonade wine." One of his books bears the significant title *Attack upon "Christendom,"* and he puts the word Christendom between inverted commas to bring out the difference between it and real Christianity. "Christendom," he wrote in his *Journal*, "has mocked God and continued to mock Him— just as if to a man who is a lover of nuts, instead of bringing him one nut with a kernel, we were to bring him tons and millions of nuts—but of empty nuts, and then make this show of zeal in complying with his wish." An exaggerated way of speaking, you will say. Yes, no doubt; but perhaps it is the only kind of speech that can penetrate our defences and show them up as nothing but the flimsiest of white-washed walls.

The best thing that could happen to you and me is that we should learn to expose ourselves once again to these prophetic voices. But prophets are such uncomfortable people, so disturbing to our complacency! "O Jerusalem, Jerusalem," our Lord said, "thou that killest the prophets, and stonest them which are sent unto thee!" Well, we do not always kill them, but we so often do our best to silence them, or at least to ignore them.

But is there then in your life and mine no whitewash that needs thus to be exposed? Is there no part of the front I show to the world that is merely a whited wall? Is there no insincerity behind the profession I make? Do I live up to my own acknowledged standards? Do I practise what I preach? Do I demand no more of others than I exemplify in myself? It is only by submitting myself to a thorough discipline of self-examination that I can come near to returning the true answers to these questions, because a long habit of deceiving others has led me in the end to deceive myself. I am taken in by my own whitewash. And that is why God in His mercy has always provided, and still provides, His Church with prophets; "God," writes St. Paul, "hath set some in the church, first apostles, secondarily prophets . . ."; that may help us to a self-examination such as we could not have accomplished without their aid. It is recorded that the saintly Bishop Gore, when being congratulated in his old age on the honoured place he had won for himself in the esteem of his Christian brethren, replied by saying, "Yes, I've been a pretty successful hypocrite, haven't I?" Are you shocked that he should have said that? Do you think it brings him down nearer to your level and mine? I think rather that it raises him above us, as showing that he had taken the prophetic teaching to heart in a way that we are seldom prepared to do.

What applies to our individual religious lives applies also to the corporate life of the Church. Ezekiel and Amos, Tertullian, Savonarola and Luther, were just as much aware of that as of the other. It applies to our congregational life, and to the Church everywhere, and to the front which Christianity as a whole is presenting to the contemporary world. Are there no whitewashed walls there? Outsiders insist that there are. They suspect that the front we show to the world is largely only a façade. But I think these outsiders often find the whitewash in the wrong places. In the past it was not the cavillers outside the Church, but the prophets within it, like Ezekiel and Luther and the rest, who exposed its real hypocrisies and corruptions. Can it not be so again today? Cannot the Church forearm itself against attacks from without by allowing the voice of prophecy to be once more heard within her walls, by showing such an awareness of her own deficiencies as will stop the mouths of her detractors, stealing their thunder? Cannot we Christians again learn to stand before these others, not as passing muster any more than they before the judgement of Almighty God, but only as better understanding our own sinfulness and our own need of mercy, and therefore as placing our sole reliance upon divine forgiveness through the merits of our Blessed Lord? Not as though we had already attained, or were already perfect; yet let this be our constant prayer:

> Dear Master, in whose life I see
> All that I would but fail to be,
> Let Thy clear light for ever shine,
> To shame and guide this life of mine.
>
> Though what I dream and what I do
> In my weak days are always two,
> Help me, oppressed by things undone,
> O Thou, whose deeds and dreams were one!

14

PASCAL AND ST. PAUL

For we know in part, and we prophesy in part. But when that which is perfect is come, then that which is in part shall be done away. . . . For now we see through a glass, darkly; but then face to face: now I know in part; but then shall I know even as also I am known. And now abideth faith, hope, charity, these three; but the greatest of these is charity. Follow after charity.

I CORINTHIANS XIII, 9—XIV, I.

"MAN," wrote Blaise Pascal, "is only a reed, the most feeble thing in nature; but he is a thinking reed. The entire universe does not need to arm itself in order to crush him. A vapour, a drop of water suffices to kill him. But if the universe *should* crush him, man would still be more noble than that which kills him, because he knows the advantage the universe has over him and knows that he must die, while the universe knows nothing of this. Thus," Pascal concludes, "our whole dignity consists in thinking." Now thinking is nothing but an attempt to understand, and surely Pascal was right in believing that the principal difference between man and the rest of creation, and the only difference in which he can take any pride, is that he alone tries to understand. The rest of creation just is what it is, but man alone seeks to understand what he is. Yet he cannot understand himself without at the same time understanding the scheme of things entire. He can know the meaning of his own existence only in proportion as he knows the meaning of all existence. For the meaning of a part consists in its relation to the meaning of the whole.

Has man then any such knowledge? Yes, says Pascal, he has, but not very much. And that also is St. Paul's answer. "We know in part," he says; "we see through a glass darkly," or, as it is better translated, "we see as in a mirror, as in a riddle"—and the only mirrors which St. Paul's Corinthian correspondents had at their disposal, and for the export of which their city was indeed famous, were made of burnished brass, so that the reflection must have been rather a dim one. Both writers thus agree that we stand somewhere between satisfying knowledge and total ignorance. "For in fact," asks Pascal, "what is man in the system of nature? He is a Nothing in comparison with the Infinite, an All in comparison with the Nothing. He is a mean between Nothing and Everything . . . This is our true state. This is what makes us incapable alike of certain knowledge and of absolute ignorance." "Nature confounds the pyrrhonists, while reason confounds the dogmatists." "Man is neither an angel on the one hand, nor a brute beast on the other." One is reminded of Alexander Pope's lines in his *Essay on Man*:

> With too much knowledge for the Sceptic side,
> With too much weakness for the Stoic's pride,
> He hangs between; in doubt to act or rest,
> In doubt to deem himself a God or Beast.

Pascal is as eloquent as St. Paul about the unsatisfactoriness of this situation. We are, he says, like beings "cast up by the tempest upon an unknown island," when there is so much they want to know but have no means of finding out. It may perhaps occur to us that we have now found out a great many things that were unknown to Pascal, and still more things that were unknown to St. Paul; and perhaps during the recent Geophysical Year we may have found out some further things. Yet it is important to realise that the kind of things we have discovered and are every day continuing to discover do not even in the least degree abate the ignorance of which St. Paul and Pascal were thinking. They leave our fundamental human situation exactly as they found it. They answer none of the questions we most want to put. They bring us no step nearer to that perfect knowledge of which St. Paul here speaks and for which he so ardently longs. They do nothing to enlighten us concerning the meaning either of our own existence or of all existence. They offer no further guidance as to why we are here, or what we are supposed to do, now that we *are* here. So far as we do know what to do, they can perhaps suggest to us certain better ways of doing it; and without altering at all the essential conditions of our life on earth, they can perhaps make us a little more comfortable while we have to bear with these; like the treatment which my doctor recently prescribed to me for a stiffness in my joints, and when I asked him "Will it cure it?", he replied, "No, it will only soothe it."

But we do not want to be soothed. We do not want to forget. Man may be only a reed, the feeblest thing in nature, but he is a thinking reed; and since that is his only claim to dignity, he must on no account forfeit it. Therefore we should rejoice that we live in an age whose leading intellectual spokesmen are no longer content with anodynes and facile solutions, but are anxious to look the tragic facts of our human predicament straight in the face. You remember the lines:

> Could man be drunk forever
>   With liquor, love and fights,
> Lief should I rouse at morning
>   And lief lie down of nights.

But men at whiles are sober
And think by fits and starts,
And if they think, they fasten
Their hands upon their hearts.

Our age is one that really does think by fits and starts. Our leading scientists of today would be the first to deny that their discoveries are such as to pierce the veil of our ultimate ignorance, the last to claim that their inventions have altered our ultimate prospects. Our leading philosophers are equally realist, repudiating the idealist constructions of their comparatively recent predecessors. Their modesty and self-abnegation may perhaps be carried to an extreme, so that philosophy now seems to be engaged in arguing itself out of existence. But so far as it embodies an awareness of the ultimate mystery with which we are surrounded, and a frank recognition of the tragic sense of life, it represents a real gain. Plato said long ago that "those who rightly engage in philosophy study only dying and death," and I find it a hopeful thing that our contemporary thinkers are so unblinking in their contemplation of this "last enemy," as St. Paul called it; one of the most influential among them (Martin Heidegger) defining our human existence as "an existence towards death," and declaring that the only true basis for understanding our life as a whole is to see every moment of it in the context of the death which awaits us. Pascal constantly protests that his work as an apologist for the Christian faith cannot make any headway with those who try to blink the immensity of our human ignorance or the depth of our human misery.

Yet Pascal believes that when these facts are recognised, there is hope of something else being recognised also. For Pascal is neither a complete agnostic nor a radical pessimist. He claimed, you remember, to stand midway between the agnostics and the dogmatists. We might almost say that he is an agnostic towards the dogmatists and a dogmatist towards the agnostics. Man, he holds, "is incapable alike of certain knowledge and of absolute ignorance." "What a contradiction," he writes elsewhere in characteristic style, "is man! Judge of all things, imbecile worm of the earth; depositary of truth, a sink of ignorance and error; the pride and refuse of the universe!" How like that is again to Pope, who wrote in the following century:

> Sole judge of Truth, in endless Error hurl'd:
> The glory, jest and riddle of the world!

We cannot then say that we know nothing—or nothing that will relieve our misery. "We know in part," as St. Paul says, though it may be a very small part—even infinitesimally small in comparison with a perfect knowledge, so that St. Paul can also say, "When that which is perfect is come, then that which is in part shall be done away." Yet after all faith is farther removed from total ignorance than it is from perfect knowledge; and seeing in a mirror dimly is less like not seeing at all than it is like seeing face to face.

So here also I must agree with Pascal and St. Paul. I cannot say that I know nothing, that I have no clue to the mystery of life. It would be dishonest of me to say this. I know, for instance, that I am under obligation to love my neighbour as myself, to give as much thought and care to his good as I do to my own. This is contrary to my natural inclination: it is in many ways a most unwelcome piece of knowledge, and I constantly find myself trying to suppress it. But all such attempts are futile, because in my heart of hearts I know it to be true. In spite of myself, I am more certain of this than of anything science or philosophy could tell me. Yet it is a very mysterious piece of knowledge, because somehow it could not possibly exist in my mind all by itself. I am under obligation; but who or what is it that obliges me? I clearly know that I am under authority, and have no right to do just as I like; but under whose authority? Well, you remember that He who said, "Thou shalt love thy neighbour as thyself," said first, "Thou shalt love the Lord thy God"; and I know that this first commandment also is one that I must obey. And not only so, but I know also that the two pieces of knowledge are most closely interconnected—that the love of God is somehow contained in the love of my neighbour, and the love of my neighbour in the love of God. To put it otherwise, I know that the love of my neighbour would not be the sort of love that is required of me, if it had not some such overtone as is meant when we speak of the love of God. Altruism can be a very sorry thing, if it is not pervaded by a sense of the Holy, by a sense that my life is a sacred trust. In knowing that I must love and serve my human brethren, I know also that I was put here to do this very thing, so that I have here a clue to the meaning of my own life, but some clue also to the meaning of the universal system in which I am enmeshed. It would thus be quite dishonest of me to say that I have no clue to the mystery, and am accordingly free to follow my own sweet will.

A slender enough clue, you will perhaps say, and it would indeed be slender if it had received no further embodiment, if the Word I thus hear spoken to me had not been made flesh. But, as the writer of the Epistle to the Hebrews puts it, "God who in many and various ways spoke in time past to our fathers by the prophets has in these last days spoken unto us by a Son." Some theologians of our time have indeed persuaded themselves that, if this had not happened, they would be without *any* clue to the mystery or *any* knowledge of the obligation under which they now know themselves to stand. I could not myself assert this with confidence, but I do know that in fact it is the constraint of Jesus Christ from which I find it most impossible to escape. I just cannot read the Gospel story without knowing that I am being sought out in love, that I am at the same time being called to life's most sacred task and being offered life's highest prize. For it is the love God has shown me in Christ that constrains me to the love of my fellow men. If there be someone who is aware of no such constraint, I cannot of course hope to make him aware of it by speaking these few sentences. That would require, not so much a more elaborate argument as something quite different from any argument. But I am not now arguing. I am only confessing, and I know there are many who will want to confess with me.

I know in part, then, but sometimes it seems a distressingly small part. The reflection in the mirror is often tantalisingly dim. Clouds and thick darkness still surround the mystery. I pine for a clearer vision, as St. Paul and Pascal pined for it; but I know also, as they did, that the appointed conditions of our human life are such that I must continue to do without it. Yet I must not grumble at this dispensation of things. No doubt it has a purpose to serve. It is indeed a sore trial, but perhaps that is just what it was meant to be—it was meant to try me out.

But already in his famous sermon, "Upon the Ignorance of Man," Bishop Butler had put this forward as a cardinal truth. Our condition in this world, he says, is a school of self-discipline, and there would have been insufficient opportunity for the exercise of such discipline, if we had what he calls complete sensible evidence of the truth of our faith.

"The strict discharge of our duty," he writes, "with less sensible evidence, does imply in it a better character than the same diligence in discharge of it, upon more sensible evidence. This fully accounts for and explains that assertion of our Saviour, 'Blessed are they that have not seen, and yet have believed'.

. . . If to acquire knowledge were our proper end, we should indeed be but poorly provided: but if somewhat else be our business and duty, we may, notwithstanding our ignorance, be well enough furnished for it; and the observation of our ignorance may be of assistance to us in the discharge of it."

Meanwhile, says St. Paul, and in the absence of fuller enlightenment, three things remain to us—faith, hope, and charity or love. By faith we know in part, discerning the truth dimly as in a mirror. By hope we hold fast to the vision of a more perfect knowledge which is like to that by which we ourselves are known. By love we serve one another. These three constitute between them the whole appointed filling of our earthly existence, as we stand here in the mist, in the twilight, as Butler calls it, between knowledge and ignorance, "placed on this isthmus of a middle state." And which of the three is the greatest? If we had had to guess at St. Paul's answer, we should probably have said faith; for has he not been called the Apostle of Faith, and is not faith the key word of his theology? But no, when he puts the question to himself straight, he says firmly, "The greatest of these is charity." For "though I have all faith, so that I could remove mountains, and have not charity, I am nothing." And Pascal agrees with him when in one of his *Pensées* he writes:

All bodies together and all minds together, and all their productions, are not worth the least movement of charity, which is of an infinitely higher order. From all bodies together we cannot obtain one little thought; for that is impossible and of another order. From all bodies and all minds together we cannot produce a movement of true charity; that is impossible and of still another order, this time a supernatural one, because 'all charity is of God.'

Therefore, concludes St. Paul, "Follow after charity." "Follow after love."

PART III

THE SUBSTANCE OF THE FAITH

15

THE MEANING OF THE
INCARNATION

God was in Christ, reconciling the world unto himself.
II CORINTHIANS V, 19.

THIS is the declaration on which the Christian religion is founded. We call it the doctrine of the Incarnation, and there is no question that it is the central doctrine of the Christian faith. It consists, as you see, in the conjunction of two names—those of God and Christ. "God was in Christ, reconciling the world unto himself." This doctrine, then, can only be understood if we understand *first* what we mean by God, *then* what we mean by Christ, and *lastly* what is implied in the conjunction of the two names. These, then, will be the three heads of my discourse.

First, then, what do we mean by God? I think the best answer we can give is to say that *God is He with whom we have ultimately to do.* He is the final underlying reality of life and the world. Have you ever reflected how little *reality* there is in the life of most of us; how seldom, in the life of an ordinary day, the average man touches the underlying reality of things at all—how seldom he faces things as they really are? The so-called realities with which he is dealing are at most realities of a relative kind. If, for instance, he be a man of business, then his practical ultimates are the pound sterling and the gold standard and the Bank of England and the Stock Exchange. He seldom gets nearer reality than these things. Well, you may say, he might be a great deal farther off. After all, these things *are* pretty stable. They are pillars of our national life, they lie at the root of all our institutions. They are the foundations on which our civilisation is built. But our civilisation itself—how much reality is there in that? Whatever else reality means, it means something that is not subject to corruption, over which time has no power, something that is going to last for ever. Yet surely nobody seriously supposes that our civilization is going to last *for ever*.

> Troy Town is covered up with weeds,
>   The rabbits and the pismires brood
> On broken gold, and shards, and beads
>   Where Priam's ancient palace stood.

> Last week in Babylon,
>   Last night in Rome,
> Morning—and in the crush
>   Under Paul's dome. . . .

When other systems and civilizations have risen and decayed, do we still cheat ourselves with the illusion that ours alone is immortal? Will Time, the old Gipsy man, keep his caravan stationary under Paul's dome for ever and a day? Sometimes when we have felt most secure and had settled ourselves down most comfortably, something has come hurtling in to our tidy little system of things from a region altogether beyond our ken and beyond our control, and then we knew that we were face to face with reality at last!

Or take the case of the scholar. It must be confessed that the scholar is just as likely as the man of business to shut himself up in a little world of his own choosing and to nourish in himself the illusion that his little chosen world is immortal and indestructible and the only world there is.

The book-lined walls of the study are as often taken for the *flammantia moenia mundi* as are the walls of the counting-house. We are engrossed in our favourite studies and researches and forget that there is any reality beyond them—until suddenly it breaks in upon us bleakly. I remember one student who never really grasped the fact that there was a world outside his study walls until one day the postman handed him a letter saying that his father had failed in business and that he must now work with his hands for his bread. I remember another who was suddenly faced with reality in a very different form—in the shape of a fellow human being with whom it would be his duty to live for many years in intimate daily association and yet whose temperament seemed to him to be what is called incompatible with his own—and that was something that was not dreamed of in his philosophy.

But it is the same no matter what our walk in life may be. How little reality there is in our lives! How seldom we face things as they really are! We accept a few familiar things as the fixed points round which our lives revolve, and we seldom look beyond them to see what they are fixed to, and how long they are likely to remain fixed, or even whether they are really fixed at all or only seem so to us who are carried round along with them. We do not look beyond them because we are afraid. That is what is wrong with most of us—we are afraid of reality. We do not feel equal to its demands. We do not want to be shaken into so inconvenient an awareness. This universe, says Dr. L. P. Jacks in one of his books, "is ill adapted to the fearful and the unbelieving; but most exquisitely adapted to the loyal, the loving and the brave." I think we all know in our hearts that that is what reality is like, and so we do our best to escape from it—and our escape consists in selecting a few cosy and seductive things that have some small degree of reality and stability and permanence in them, and building out of them a little private world for ourselves—as we built playhouses when we were children. But one thing is certain, and that is that *some* day, be it soon or late, this reality that we are trying to evade will directly confront us and take no further refusal: "Thou fool, this night shall thy soul be required of thee: then whose shall those things be, which thou hast provided?" "Lest coming suddenly He find you sleeping." This reality then is what we mean by God. *God is He with whom you and I have in the last resort to reckon*—it is the only definition we can give.

> Our little systems have their day,
>   They have their day and cease to be.
>   They are but broken lights of Thee,
> And Thou, O Lord, art more than they.

But now secondly, what do we mean by Christ? Ah, now we are on different ground and the answer is much easier. This question is not to be answered by any kind of abstract philosophy but only by a *story*; for here is no unsolved mystery of ultimate reality but One who dwelt among ourselves in the flesh, full of grace and truth. You know the story well, and I am not going to retell it for you but only to remind you of it in the fewest possible words. When you and I say "Jesus Christ," we have in mind a life of a very definite and particular kind that was once lived out on this old planet of ours. What kind of life was it then? Was it the life of a prince, an imperial Caesar, born with a silver spoon in his mouth, ministered unto from the cradle to the grave, swaying his thousands of minions by the might of his sceptre, living out his days in luxury, surrounded by gold and rare metals and precious stones? Or again was it the life of some great hero of romance, leading victorious armies into battle and meeting, perhaps, an honourable death in the field? Or once again was it the life of a philosopher, cloistered in his academic seclusion from the noisy world, lapped in leisure and surrounded by his beloved books and papers, and dying at a great age safely in his bed?

No, it was none of these but something amazingly, disconcertingly different from them all. No, Jesus Christ was only the son of a common artisan's wife, born (so rumour had it) in a horse's stall, spending His youth in a carpenter's shop; and the life He lived was a life of the greatest possible simplicity, the greatest possible unobtrusiveness and meekness and humility; a life of strangely outgoing quality in which self bulked very little; a life spent, as a follower once summed it up, "in doing good and in healing all that were oppressed of the devil"; a ministering life rather than one that sought to be ministered unto; a life passed for the most part not among the whole but among the sick, and not among righteous men but among publicans and sinners; a life that gave to him that asked from it and never turned away from the borrower; a life grounded from first to last not on requital but on forgiveness, not on getting but on giving, not on self-saving but on self-spending; a life that at the last readily gave itself up to death in order that others might live more abundantly. I think that as we look at this life and put together as best we may all the incidents and aspects of it, two main characteristics stand out—first its outgoing quality and then the reliance it places on love alone. *That*, then, is what we mean when we pronounce the name of Jesus Christ—we mean the passion to redeem and the determination to do it by suffering love and not by any kind of violence; a love that suffereth long and is kind, that seeketh not her own and is not easily provoked, that beareth all things, believeth all things, hopeth all things, endureth all things.

We have now before us the meaning of the two names that we linked together in the doctrine of the Incarnation.

The name of God stands for the final reality with which you and I are face to face. The name of Christ stands for a particular kind of life—a life of outgoing and suffering love. And now the answer to our question lies in our hands. To what exactly (that was the question) are you and I committing ourselves when in the recitation of our Christian creed we link the two names together and affirm the Godhead of Christ? There can be no doubt now about the answer. We are committing ourselves to the declaration that in that life which Jesus lived and in that death which He died lies the secret of the universe. We are taking our stand upon the solemn asseveration that the things the Man of Nazareth stood for are the most real things in all the world. We are deliberately subscribing to the faith that in the contemplation of suffering love we are face to face with the reality of things at last. Love, we are declaring, is omnipotent and Omnipotence is love! As it was put by somebody very long ago, "He that loveth his brother abideth in the light. . . . But he that hateth his brother is in darkness, and walketh in darkness, and knoweth not whither he goeth, because that darkness hath blinded his eyes."

Ah, did we think, you and I, that this confession of the Godhead of Christ was a confession that we might lightly take upon our lips? Did we think that when we intoned the words, ". . . And in Jesus Christ his only Son our Lord," we were committing ourselves to nothing practical but only to some remote theoretical formula? Did we think that this Christian creed was a harmless, spineless thing, and that we could repeat it like a piece of mummery without any danger of disturbance to our smug and pampered lives? I tell you No! I tell you that no other dogma that has ever been published in the world is so severely, so terribly practical as this one. I tell you that no commitment which men have ever taken on their lips is so exacting and testing as this one, or makes such inexorable demands upon the daily conduct of their lives! Do not lightly confess to this belief, then, but think well before you take it on your lips. For to declare with our lips that in the Christ-life resides the final secret of the universe, and then to go out into the world to live an un-Christlike life; to declare with our lips that in this outgoing and suffering love we see the most real of all realities, and then ourselves to live a life of self-centred indulgence; to recite with the great congregation our belief that in these deeds of long-suffering humility we see the eternal God plainly revealed, and then ourselves to show haughtiness and unforgiving malice; to put our names to the solemn asseveration that Omnipotence itself is love, and then to doubt love's potency to surmount the first little hurdle which it is called upon to face—what possible contradiction could be more insupportable than that, and how can the man who is guilty of it retain even a shred of his self-respect?

The doctrine of the Incarnation is often felt to be a difficult belief, and indeed it is a difficult belief. To confess the Godhead of Christ can never be an easy thing for anybody. But I am quite sure that its greatest difficulty is not theoretical but practical. Indeed I should say that the way to tell whether a man *really* believes in the Divinity of Christ is not to listen to his verbal professions, but to look at his deeds. So I would put to every one this most searching question, which I put also solemnly to myself, and upon the answer to which, as I believe, everything depends: Would the people who see you daily, and with whom you have most to do, be able to guess, even if you had not told them, that you believe in the Divinity of Christ?

Such is the challenge which in every age the doctrine of the Incarnation has brought to all who confess its truth. And yet it has brought them something else too—it has brought them a promise and an assurance and a hope. Christianity has always been a religion that first casts men down and then lifts them up. It begins by challenging us unto self-condemnation, but it ends by reassuring us unto eternal blessedness. And if I would be true to my high topic, it is on this note of promise and assurance that I must bring to a close what I have had to say. For if it be true that God was in Christ, if it be true that in this Christ-life the very life of God is plainly revealed and that this outgoing redemptive passion, this suffering and long-suffering love, are indeed the very pillars on which the spiritual universe is built, then this means not only that in this way we must deal with one another but that *in this way we are being dealt with ourselves*. We are surrounded by that very love whereunto we are constrained. We are not asked to do anything better for our brothers than God is all the time doing for us. Christ does not command us to go out after other lost sheep without assuring us that God is all the time out after ourselves. He does not ask us to forgive our neighbour's trespasses without assuring us that our Heavenly Father is ready and waiting to forgive our own—if only we open our hearts to His love. God is in Christ challenging—aye, but He is also in Christ reconciling—reconciling an erring world unto Himself. And now for that blessed reconciliation, and for all it means to men like you and me who know we can never properly stand up to the challenge, let us ascribe unto God the Father and unto Christ the Son all honour and glory and merit throughout all ages, world without end.

16

TIBERIUS AND JOHN

Now in the fifteenth year of the reign of Tiberius Caesar, Pontius Pilate being governor of Judaea, and Herod being tetrarch of Galilee, and his brother Philip tetrarch of Ituraea and of the region of Trachonitis, and Lysanias tetrarch of Abilene, Annas and Caiaphas being the high priests, the word of God came unto John the son of Zacharias in the wilderness. ST. LUKE III, 1–2.

HERE is a wonderful assemblage of names—Tiberius, Pontius Pilate, Herod, Philip, Lysanias, Annas and Caiaphas. Tiberius the great Roman Emperor; Pilate his high-ranking civil servant as Procurator of Judaea; the Jewish half-brothers Herod Antipas and Philip who were allowed by the Romans to exercise a dependent rule in the regions of Galilee and Ituraea respectively; Lysanias with a like commission in Abilene; Annas and Caiaphas, high priests of the Temple in Jerusalem. But for St. Luke all these resounding names serve only to fix a date in the life of John the son of Zacharias. And who was this John? He was as uncouth and unkempt a figure as you could well imagine; a nomad of the desert, lean and long-haired, wearing only a garment of camel's hair, eating only of what he could find in the desert—locust beans and wild honey, drinking no wine but only brackish water from holes in the sand. Surely there is something wrong with St. Luke's sense of values, that he should thus pass over the names of kings and em-

perors and governors and princes of the Church, using them
only to fix the year in which this grotesque oriental wanderer emerged from the wilderness of Judaea to appear by
the banks of the Jordan river.

Well, let us consider. There were many worse Roman
emperors than Tiberius. He was in many respects a good
ruler, conscientious and untiring in the service of the state,
clear-sighted in his policies, just and equitable in his dealings. Yet in all his personal relationships he was the most
lamentable of failures. One historian has written that "it
is a question whether he ever liked or was liked by a single
human being." Secretive, remote and unlovable from the
beginning, he finally became, in Pliny's words, "the gloomiest of mankind," retiring for the last eleven years of his
life to the island of Capri, where people still speak of him,
and where his mind became haunted almost to madness
with superstitious fears. Then Pontius Pilate, owing his appointment to Tiberius, and in some ways perhaps an able
administrator, trying to do his best in a difficult situation,
torn as he was between the desire to please his Roman
masters and the necessity of appeasing the Jewish priests
and populace; but failing utterly when his great test came.
Pilate compromised with his own conscience. He took water
and washed his hands, but the stain was not removed.
And his only memorial to all generations is in the words
that have been repeated by countless thousands every day
for nearly two thousand years: "crucified under Pontius
Pilate." Then Herod, who may also have been an able ruler,
but whose name is chiefly known to us for a similar com-
promise with his conscience. When Herodias asked him at
his birthday feast to serve up John's head upon a platter,
he was, we are told, exceeding sorry, but that did not prevent him from giving the horrible order to gratify his
paramour. Then Philip, his half-brother, who is remembered

chiefly as the rightful husband of this same Herodias, whom Herod had immorally and illegally taken to himself. Then Lysanias, of whom we know nothing but his name and his high office. Then Annas and Caiaphas, the adroit and worldly-minded Sadducean priests who secured trumped-up charges sufficient to send Jesus to His death.

All these were men of high place and worldly authority, and all were spiritually insignificant and morally contemptible. But unto John the desert wanderer came the word of God. Think what that means, if you would understand St. Luke's scale of values. Mankind has always had the sense that there was a meaning in human life more profound than any that appeared upon the surface. They have felt that our life on earth must be a vain show, "stale, flat and unprofitable," unless some light could be shed upon it from beyond its own frontiers, and they have waited with eager longing for such a light to be revealed. John came to herald the appearance of that light. He brought men a word from God; a word from beyond the curtain of time and sense, a word that was more than the fumbling words of men, a word bearing directly upon our deepest human concern, a word of final release from our fundamental human predicament.

Yet, as we read in the Gospel, John himself "was not that Light, but was sent to bear witness of that Light." John came with a word, and it was a word from God, but he came only to prepare the way for the Word made flesh. And none knew that better than John himself. "I am only a voice," he said, "the voice of one crying in the wilderness, saying, Prepare." "After me there cometh one mightier than I, the thong of whose sandals I am not worthy to stoop down and untie." "He must increase, but I must decrease." That means that the great event the date of which St. Luke is here concerned to fix is not the advent of John, but the advent of Him whose way John came to prepare—the advent of our Lord and Saviour Jesus Christ. And actually this is the only fixed date we have in gospel chronology. We know from other sources that the fifteenth year of the reign of Tiberius Caesar corresponded to the year 28–29 A.D. in our system of reckoning, and from that we are able to calculate certain other dates in the life of our Lord.

I say "our system of reckoning," but remember what that means. We now reckon all the dates in the history of mankind either backwards or forwards from the birth of Him whose appearance in Galilee John came to announce. At the head of every business and private letter written this day here in far-away Scotland there will appear the mysterious figure 195–. But that means that we are accepting St. Luke's estimate of relative values. It means that we are paying at least lip-service to the centrality of Christ. Every time we write that figure we are tacitly acknowledging that the most significant thing about any other event in history is whether it happened before or after the event of His coming—whether it is B.C. or A.D., as we say. We forget all about Tiberius and Herod and the rest of them, and we write only the words, "In the year of our Lord 195–."

When the modern secular world thinks of history, it is apt to picture it as an upward sloping line, starting very low down very long ago, gradually rising upward until the present time, and destined to continue rising towards a consummation still to be attained. But the picture in the Christian mind, and which has dominated Christian civilization, is something more like an hour-glass, or like one of these old-fashioned glasses for timing the cooking of an egg, which I used to see in the Highlands in my boyhood—the sand running through a narrow neck between two bulbs. One bulb would represent all that went before Christ's

Advent—the era of promise; the other would represent all that has come after—the era of fulfilment; and the narrow neck would represent the Advent itself, through which all the sand of history must pass if mankind is to find the release that our Lord came to bestow.

This means also that the most significant fact about your life and mine today is the relation in which it stands to the advent of Jesus Christ. Nothing else about us really matters at all as compared with that. The saddest thing that could be said about any one of us would be that we were living in the nineteen hundred and fiftieth year of our Lord, and yet were living as if our Lord had not yet come. When the Jacobins of 1792 declared that they had given up the Christian faith and set up the Goddess of Reason in the Pantheon at Paris, they set out at the same time to reform the calendar, counting the year one as from that date. That was at least honest. But the sad thing is when those who continue to acknowledge Christ in their calendar deny Him the service of their heart. For I think we all know that the events that began to transpire in Galilee in the fifteenth year of the reign of Tiberius Caesar were either the turning-point of human history or were of no significance at all. The tremendous claim that our Lord made for Himself is either true or a piece of irresponsible absurdity. Remember some of His words. "All things are delivered unto me of my Father: and no man knoweth the Son, but the Father; neither knoweth any man the Father, save the Son, and he to whomsoever the Son will reveal him. Come unto me, all ye that labour and are heavy laden, and I will give you rest." If He spoke these words falsely, then we must dismiss Him altogether from our minds, as did the Jacobins; but if He spoke them truly, then we must surrender our whole lives to Him and make every other loyalty subservient to His imperious claim.

It is true that there have been those who, without altogether rejecting His claim, have tried to trifle with it, scaling it down to something they might be able to accept without too radical a readjustment of their existing outlook and behaviour. But mankind as a whole has been more clear-sighted. Men have for the most part understood, even when unwilling to act on the understanding, that with Christ it must be all or nothing. It was not so many generations after the death of Tiberius that the Empire he ruled began to have some appreciation of this. Do you remember Matthew Arnold's dramatic lines?

> She heard it, the victorious West,
>   In crown and sword array'd!
> She felt the void which mined her breast,
>   She shiver'd and obey'd.
>
> She veil'd her eagles, snapp'd her sword,
>   And laid her sceptre down;
> Her stately purple she abhorr'd
>   And her imperial crown.
>
> She broke her flutes, she stopp'd her sports,
>   Her artists could not please;
> She tore her books, she shut her courts,
>   She fled her palaces;
>
> Lust of the eye and pride of life
>   She left it all behind,
> And hurried, torn with inward strife,
>   The wilderness to find.
>
> Tears wash'd the trouble from her face!
>   She chang'd into a child!
> 'Mid weeds and wrecks she stood—a place
>   Of ruin—but she smiled!

If you and I are among those who acknowledge the true significance of the events that began to happen in the fifteenth year of the reign of Tiberius Caesar, and if on the strength of that acknowledgement we claim to be disciples of Christ, then let me conclude by suggesting that each of us should put two questions to himself. First, what has there been in my life this day that would not have been there, if I were not a Christian? And second, from what deeds or words or thoughts have I this day refrained, from which I would not have refrained, if I were not a disciple of Him whose way John the son of Zacharias came to prepare in the fifteenth year of the reign of Tiberius Caesar, Pontius Pilate being governor of Judaea, and Herod being tetrarch of Galilee, and his brother Philip tetrarch of Ituraea, and Lysanias the tetrarch of Abilene, Annas and Caiaphas being the high priests?

17

GOD IN THREE TENSES

Grace be unto you, and peace, from him which is, and which was, and which is to come. REVELATION I, 4.

THE Book of Revelation was written just as the young Christian Church was beginning to face the first persecutions. The situation was as dark as it could be. Caesar had been proclaimed as a god, and all citizens of the Empire were expected to bow down in worship before his statue. Those who did not were not only boycotted in the marketplace, but were liable also to suffer imprisonment, banishment or martyrdom. The Christians could not thus abrogate their faith, and it looked as if the Christian Church were not going to be allowed to live. The writer of this book, who had himself been exiled to the wild island of Patmos in the Aegean, dare not mention Caesar by name, so he calls him the Beast; and he tells us in the thirteenth chapter that men were commanded to make an image of the Beast, that as many as would not worship the Beast were threatened with death, that all, both small and great, rich and poor, free and bond, were made to receive a mark on their right hands or in their foreheads, and that no man might buy or sell save that he had on him the mark of the Beast.

The purpose of St. John the Divine in writing his book is to comfort the churches of Asia Minor in this grave situation, and to strengthen them in their resolution. How does

he set out to do it? Well, I think it very significant that he
begins by wishing them grace and peace from the God who
is, and who was and who is to come, reminding them that
the God in whom Christians put their trust is a God in all
three tenses. He repeats this same reminder several times
in the course of his book. He says it again in this same first
chapter: "I am Alpha and Omega, the beginning and the
ending, saith the Lord, which is, and which was, and which
is to come." And again later on: "I heard the angel of the
waters say, Thou are righteous, O Lord, which art, and
wast, and shalt be, because thou hast judged thus."

In our own day also the Church of Christ is facing a grave
situation, a situation which in some countries has closely
resembled that of these early Christians in the age of Nero
and Domitian, when men were persecuted for the faith
that was in them. And even in our own country things are
very different from the smooth tenor of the past. Indeed
one frequently hears the remark that we are living in an
apocalyptic situation. But if that is true, then this book
of the Apocalypse, which had lately seemed to us altogether
too fanciful and remote from reality, may be expected to
take on new life for us. And especially I think it well worth
our while to reflect whether we do not at this moment
stand particularly in need of the assurance that the God
whom we worship is a God who is, a God who was, and a
God who is to come.

First, He is a God who is. He is a living God who was
never more present and active than in the present situation. That was the first thing that these Christians of the
age of persecution needed to know. The events of that age
did not *look* as if God were controlling them. Things looked
rather as if God had forgotten His own. The Christians had
been told that all things work together for good to them
that love God, but nothing at present seemed to be work-

ing for their good. From one congregation after another came the report that the faithful were being hunted down, exiled, imprisoned and slain. They tried hard to keep their faith alive through it all, yet they had a feeling of being forsaken. And now, from the lonely island of Patmos, one of those who has been thus exiled writes to them this sort of circular letter to assure them that their God is a God who is.

Is not that something of which we also need to be reminded? We all profess to believe in God, but we incline to think of Him as One who created the world long ago and now dwells in His own remote Heaven, leaving the world to look after itself. But if we think like that, then it is not God we are believing in at all. For God is He who is. He is here now. He is as literally present as you are or as I am. Here, at this moment, His is the dominating presence. Nor is He present merely to observe, but also to control. Here, at this moment, He is active among us. I am afraid that sometimes when we speak of the presence of God, we think of Him as merely "listening in." And when at a Communion Service we sing, "Be present at our table, Lord," we think of Christ only as a spectator of what is there being done, as looking down from His high Heaven at this ritual that is being transacted on earth. But that is not what He meant when He said, "Here am I in the midst of them." That is not what He meant when He said, "I will never leave you." He meant that He would be present not only to observe but as playing the most active and important part of all.

Then again, when at the close of worship we go out into the world of public events, we must remind ourselves that God and Christ are there, and that they are there not as idle onlookers but as the principal actors. That was what many Christians of the age of persecution found it so difficult to believe. It looked to them as if the course of history had at last got out of God's control. It looked as if not God but the Devil were now in the saddle and held the reins. Today we are sometimes tempted to think that once again. I fear there is a good deal of defeatism within our churches at present. The forces of evil, we say, now hold the initiative, and are gaining ground every day. But what this book has to say to us is that the forces of evil never hold the initiative, because the initiative is always with God. It is He, not they, who is the Lord of history, and ultimately directs all its movements. In the dark days of the recent war we often grumbled that the initiative was with the enemy. For most of the time between 1940 and 1944 it seemed to be Hitler who was leading the play and calling the tune. But we can now see that all the time he was being blindly driven on to his own doom. We can now begin to see that at no point had things got out of God's hands. If we think that sometimes He held the reins very lightly, perhaps that also was part of His wise purpose:— it was not really that His right hand had lost its skill or His holy arm forgotten its strength. That is perhaps easy to believe now about the events of several years ago, when the agony of them is past, but we are much slower to believe it about the events of today. Yet what the Bible assures us is not merely that right will triumph in the end, not merely that God will win the last battle, but that even now He is directing the march of events. We are asked to take courage, not because the dark clouds that shadow us will one day pass, but because even now they are "big with mercy." God is a God who is.

Second, He is a God who was. This is something that the Bible everywhere emphasises. Have you ever realised that the Bible is essentially a history book? That is one respect in which it differs from the sacred books of all the other

religions. These all read like textbooks of philosophy or
theosophy or mythology or cosmology or, if you will, theology; but the Bible reads much more like a textbook of history. It is all the time concerned with the meaning of
events that have happened in space and time. There is a
prologue in heaven and a postlude in heaven, but in between it is all concerned with the action of God in time
and place. No ancient people were so conscious of their past
history as were the Hebrews under the guidance of the
prophetic teaching, and the reason why they attached so
much importance to it was just that they believed God to
have been the principal actor throughout it all. Think how
many of the hymns they sang—the hymns collected in our
own Book of Psalms—are simply a recital of God's past
dealings with His people. "We have heard with our ears,
O God, our fathers have told us, what work thou didst in
their days, in the times of old. How thou didst drive out the
heathen with thy hand" . . . and so on. "I have considered
the days of old, the years of ancient times . . . I will remember the works of the Lord: surely I will remember thy
wonders of old. I will meditate also on all thy work, and
talk of thy doings. . . . Thou leddest thy people like a
flock by the hand of Moses and Aaron."

We men are creatures of time. Our lives are lived in time,
but the only bit of time we can command is each thin and
winged moment as it passes. I am quite helpless as regards
the past, even as regards my own past. I can do nothing whatever about it. I cannot change it by so much as a hair's
breadth. And with the more distant past you and I never
had anything to do. When the world was created, we were
not there. When Israel came out of Egypt, we were not
there. When empire succeeded empire in the ancient world,
we were not there. When Scotland became a nation, we
were not there. Yet it is these events of the past and a multi-

tude of others like them, that have fixed our destiny, de-
termining our lot, marking the bounds of our habitation,
and the narrow limits of our opportunity, at the point at
which we have now been washed up on the shoals of time.

But though we were not there, God was there. The God
who is is also the God who was. And once again, He was
not there merely to observe, but as the principal actor in
the great drama, working out His eternal purpose as year
succeeded year. If we did not believe this, if we took the
pagan view of history and regarded it as merely a haphazard
succession of discrete events, one thing after another, without a plot and without a plan, our lives would be robbed
of all real meaning—"a tale told by an idiot, full of sound
and fury, signifying nothing." And as to our present sufferings, all we could do would be to grin and bear them—and
I fear it would be rather a vacant grin. But if we believe in
a God who not only is but also was, if He who is present
with us now, as we worship in His sanctuary, is also the
Ancient of Days, with whom a thousand years are as one
day and one day as a thousand years, then at once our lives
take on a solemn meaning, we are spurred on to significant
action, and we are given something to hold on to even in
our sufferings. That was why St. John the Divine reminded
the Christians of the first persecution that their God is a
God who was.

Finally, He is a God who will be, a God who is to come.
I said that the Bible differs from the sacred books of all
other religions in its concern with history. No other people
ever meditated on the days of old as the Hebrews did. And
yet I should say that the Bible's favourite tense is not the
past but the future. Some people live in the past because
they think the future has little to offer them; but the Bible's
concern with the past is of such a kind as to throw its
thought forward into the future. Every Biblical writer be-

lieves that "the best is yet to be." "No other religion before Christianity," writes Dean Inge, "ever erected hope into a moral virtue"; but in the New Testament it is made to be one of the three leading virtues, side by side with faith and love. And all this is because the Bible believes that the future is in God's hands; not in our hands, for then we should make a sorry mess of it; not in the Devil's hands, for then he would lead us to destruction; not at the mercy of any historical determinism leading us blindly forward, for then life would be without meaning; but in the hands of One who is preparing something better than eye has seen or ear heard or than has entered into the heart of man to conceive.

Nowadays I hear and read many gloomy prognostications about the future. What sort of world is it, people ask, into which our children are going to be born, or into which those now young are going to grow up? Well, when St. John the Divine wrote his book, the prospects for the immediate future were even darker than they are now. And St. John had no illusions about it. Read his book and see. He was prepared for terrors far greater than even the atomic bomb. He did not know what was going to happen next. But he did know how it was all going to turn out in the end. He remembered his Lord's words, "Brother shall deliver up brother to death, and the father the child . . . and ye shall be hated of all men for my name's sake; but he that endureth to the end shall be saved." And he echoes these words when he writes himself, "Fear none of these things which thou shalt suffer: behold, the devil shall cast some of you into prison, that ye may be tried; and ye shall have tribulation ten days: be thou faithful unto death, and I will give thee a crown of life."

Must not we also echo these words? We cannot tell what the coming years will bring us. "We know not what is coming on the earth." Though the immediate foreground of the future is clear enough, so that we know well enough where our immediate duty lies, and have light enough to take the next step, yet the middle distance is terribly dark and foreboding. But because we know that the God who was, and who is, is also the God that will be, we need have no ultimate fear. Because the same Power who has led us in the past, and who is present with us now, holds also the keys of the future, the best is yet to be; he that endureth to the end shall be saved, and the things that cannot be shaken will remain. Let us remember in the words of the paraphrase:

> Nor death nor life, nor earth nor hell,
>   Nor time's destroying sway,
> Can e'er efface us from His heart
>   Or make His love decay.
>
> Each future period *that* will bless,
>   As it has blessed the past;
> He lov'd us from the first of time;
>   He loves us to the last.

18

JESUS CHRIST THE SAME

Jesus Christ the same yesterday, and to day, and for ever.
HEBREWS XIII, 8.

THESE words were written at a time when Jesus Christ might still have been living, if His life had not been cut off before its prime; but actually they were written forty or fifty years after His death. And what they say is that Jesus Christ was the same then as He had been when He walked the Galilean ways half a century before, and that He would be the same for evermore.

Now that is a very strange thing to say about a person who has been dead for forty or fifty years. I can myself remember Queen Victoria's death. I was a schoolboy at the time and I can remember just where I was and what I was doing, when the news reached me. Only a little more than that length of time has now elapsed since that day as had elapsed since the Crucifixion when the author of the Epistle to the Hebrews put this sentence into his letter. But supposing I were now to announce as my text: "Queen Victoria, the same in my school-days, and at the present time, and for evermore." I do not know what you would think, but I hope you would be charitable enough to believe that the acoustics of the building had played me some trick and that you had not rightly heard what I had said.

The fact is that nothing either in nature or in history remains the same yesterday, today, and for ever. "You cannot step twice into the same river," said the Greek philosopher. "Times change, and we change with them," said the Latin poet. "All are of the dust, and all turn to dust again," said the Hebrew preacher. That is true of all things human and of all things under heaven, for the only being that does not change is the eternal God. The only meaning that could be given, therefore, to this sentence and of our text is that Jesus Christ was and is of the nature of God. And I need not tell you that this is exactly what the writer means to say. He has said it already in the opening paragraph of his letter. Jesus Christ, he began by saying, is "the very brightness of God's own glory and the express image of God's person." Unless this be true, this text is nonsense, and so is nearly every other text in the New Testament; and so is the whole of Christianity. Either that life of which we read in the four Gospels is the express image of God's own life, and holds in it the very brightness of God's own glory, or else it is merely a thing of the rich-treasured past like the Victorian or any other age; and in that case we had better make haste to turn our churches into museums and build up the old pagan temples once more. The things that happened in Galilee and Jerusalem nineteen hundred years ago are part of our human history, and you will find a chapter devoted to them in every history book; but the whole truth of Christianity rests on the belief that they are far more than that. It rests on the belief that in this chapter of apparently temporal events, and in this little bit of apparently mutable earthly history, we are confronted with the eternal nature of the immutable God.

Let me select only four scenes from the life of Jesus Christ and try to show how in respect of the particular characteristics displayed in them He still stands in the same relation to mankind as He did then, and how He will be the same for evermore.

1. Along the northern shore of the Lake of Galilee ran the great road from Damascus to the Mediterranean coast. At this point the richly-laden caravans passed out of the tetrarchy of Philip into the tetrarchy of Herod Antipas, and therefore there had to be a little frontier station with a customs house—as there is today at the same point between modern Syria and Palestine. The collector's name was Matthew, otherwise Levi, and this is his story: "As Jesus passed forth from thence, he saw a man, named Matthew, sitting at the receipt of custom: and he saith unto him, Follow me. And he arose and followed him." The first three Gospels tell the story in almost identical words, except that Luke says, "He *left all*, rose up, and followed him."

It is a very long time since that happened at that little frontier station between Syria and Palestine, but it has happened somewhere every day since then—just the same. It happened often while Jesus was still with men in the flesh, but it went on happening just the same after His crucifixion. It happened not only in Palestine, but went on happening all over the Mediterranean, and then it started happening in Northern Europe, and at last it started happening in my own country of Scotland—about the fourth century perhaps, and many centuries afterwards in America; and today it is happening in India, in Africa, and in the islands of the seas—just the same. There is hardly a corner of the world in which men have not heard Christ's voice calling them, and there is hardly a corner of the world in which some men have not left all and risen up and followed Him. For every one who responded to His voice as heard in the flesh, there have now been ten thousand times ten thousand who have responded to it as heard in the preaching of the Word.

There are of course many other historical figures that still affect us strongly, and many other chapters of human history that we cannot read without being enlightened in our minds or fortified in our spirits, without being strengthened in our resolution or spurred on to some further endeavour. But the particularity of *this* chapter of history is that, when men have heard it told, they have been aware of a *call*. I myself read a great deal of history, and I read the different chapters of it with mingled feelings. Sometimes I am depressed, and sometimes I am uplifted. But I cannot read about Jesus Christ without knowing that I am wanted and that it is *God* who wants me. When I hear Christ's voice, there are only two things I can do: I can stop my ears to it, or else I must rise up and follow. I suppose it is the same with others, but I can only speak for myself. I cannot read the Gospel story as I read other stories just for the lazy enjoyment of it; I cannot read it without being confronted with a choice. You see, He is the same yesterday, and today, and for ever.

II. As the traveller approaches Jerusalem from the east, the road from Jericho passes through the village of Bethany and then climbs the hill known as the Mount of Olives. Between the Mount of Olives and Jerusalem lies the deep depression of the Vale of Cedron, so that the summit of the hill discloses to the traveller a wide and sudden vista of the Holy City. When Jesus reached this spot on His last journey southwards, here is what happened: "And when he was come near, he beheld the city, and wept over it, Saying, If thou hadst known, even thou, at least in this thy day, the things which belong unto thy peace! but now they are hid from thine eyes."

That was Christ's tragic word for Jerusalem in a far-off yesterday, but do you think that no modern nation has heard Him speak the same tragic word? I wonder how many nations in the Western World today can read these words without discomfort. I think that if they want to be comfortable in their minds, and easy in their consciences, they had better keep their New Testaments closed, lest they should come upon this page. And not least ourselves. Can we of the British nation or you of the American nation read these words in this year of grace without blenching?— "If thou hadst known, even thou, at least in this thy day, the things which belong unto thy peace! but now they are hid from thine eyes." Oh yes, you say, our world has indeed an uneasy conscience, but is it Christ who makes it uneasy? The answer is that it is certainly Christ. If the Western World still professed the old paganisms and had never been stirred by the sound of Christ's name, do you think its conscience would be burdened as it is today? Do you think it would even know, in the words of James Russell Lowell, that

> Once to every man and nation
> Comes the moment to decide . . . ?

No student of history can believe it. It is Christ, and only Christ, who confronts our nation today with this tragic word of rebuke. You see, He is the same yesterday, and today, and for ever.

III. The desert comes up almost to the gates of the Galilean and Judaean cities, and on many occasions Jesus and His disciples would retire into a desert place for rest. He wanted to get away from the crowd, but sometimes the crowd followed Him. How did He then behave? The answer is given in more than one place in the Gospels, and always the same phrase is used: "He was moved with compassion toward them." And we are told that His compassion expressed itself in three ways; feeling them to be like sheep without a shepherd, He spoke to them of the Kingdom of God; He tended those who were sick; and He took measures to see that they were properly fed—even to the multiplying of the loaves and fishes.

When Christ came to Palestine long ago, He confronted men with a clearer summons, and with a sterner rebuke, than they had ever heard before, but He approached them also with a more tender compassion. The sight of a huddled crowd of mixed humanity affects different people in different ways, but Jesus could never see a crowd without being moved with compassion towards it. He knew there were few souls among them on whom life had not laid some heavy burden, and He was moved with the desire to lighten that burden. All kinds of trouble would be represented in that oriental crowd, spiritual perplexities, domestic anxieties, hunger and poverty, sickness and the fear of death; but for each Jesus had His healing word.

That was about the year 30, but it is just the same today. There are tens of thousands of our own contemporaries to bear witness that Jesus Christ is still the same. The secret of the conquest of fear, the conquest of worry, the conquest of suspense, is still to be found in His living presence. And still—

> The healing of His seamless dress
>   Is by our beds of pain;
> We touch Him in life's throng and press,
>   And we are whole again.

You see, He is the same yesterday, and today, and for ever.

IV. My last scene is of a little dinner party in one of the Galilean towns. In those days and in that part of the world men did not sit on chairs at a dinner table as we do now; they reclined on couches with their feet turned outwards. On this occasion Jesus had accepted the invitation of a Pharisee called Simon, and while they were at table, a woman of the streets, whose evil reputation was known to all, walked into the house and "stood at Jesus' feet behind him weeping." When her tears fell on His feet, she used her long hair to wipe them dry; and then she kissed His feet, and anointed them with a rare and costly perfume which she had brought with her for this purpose. Jesus allowed all this to happen without turning round, and this greatly shocked His host, who muttered something to the effect that if Jesus were really a prophet, He would have known what kind of woman this was. At last Jesus turned round to the woman and said to Simon: "Seest thou this woman? . . . Her sins, which are many, are forgiven, for she loved much"; and then to the woman He said, "Thy sins are forgiven." At this a new muttering broke out among the guests. "Who is this," they said, "that forgiveth sins also?" But Jesus said to the woman, "Thy faith hath saved thee; go in peace."

So it was often in Galilee. Men and women came to Christ having their consciences burdened with sin, and went away knowing that their sins had been forgiven. But so also it has been throughout all ages, and so it is today. This kind of thing did not stop happening when Christ died upon the Cross. Indeed it was only then that it began to spread to other lands, until now it is happening in the most distant corners of the world. For the death on the Cross was part of what made it possible, and it is to the foot of the Cross that we must all now go, if we are to hear this word of forgiveness spoken personally to ourselves. No man knows the number of those who have learned from experience that the Son of Man has power on earth to forgive sins. No man knows the number of those who have been saved by faith in the Blessed Name. No man knows the number of those who, like the woman, have come to Christ in wretchedness and gone away in peace. You see in this also, and in this above all, He is the same yesterday, and today, and for ever.

19

THE NECESSITY OF THE CROSS

For as the lightning, that lighteneth out of the one part
under heaven, shineth unto the other part under heaven;
so shall also the Son of man be in his day.
  But first must he suffer many things.
ST. LUKE XVII, 24–25.

OF ALL the things that Christ had to say to His disciples,
this was the thing they were most reluctant to believe. We
are told that He said it first after St. Peter's confession at
Caesarea Philippi, but it would seem that after that He
never ceased to say it. Indeed there is no other saying of
His that is so often repeated in the Gospels as just this
saying that the Son of Man must first suffer many things;
and the reason why He repeated it was simply that He
saw His disciples were so slow to take it in.

When Jesus began His preaching by proclaiming that
the Kingdom of God was near at hand, they were quite
ready to believe that. And when, after St. Peter's confession, He made it clear to them that He Himself was the
Son of Man who would inaugurate the Kingdom in His
own Person, they were quite ready to believe that. But
when He began to break it to them that before the Kingdom could come, the Son of Man must first suffer many
things, and be rejected, and crucified, and rise again—that
they would not and could not believe. Why this tragic
complication to damp their enthusiasm in the simple good

153

news He had brought to them? Why couldn't they march
with Him straight on to glory? During those inexpressibly
marvellous days in Nazareth and in Capernaum and by
the lakeside the Kingdom of God seemed already to have
begun. On the Mount of Transfiguration Christ seemed
already to be manifest in His glory, and they wanted to
pitch their tents for eternity there and then. When He
entered Jerusalem so triumphantly, and "the people of
the Hebrews with palms before Him went," the final triumph seemed at last to be very near. Why couldn't things
go on smoothly till all was accomplished? Would not the
people of Jerusalem flock to His standard, until soon the
new age would indeed have dawned in Israel and Jesus be
crowned as Lord of all? And especially if He was Himself
the divine Son of God, and if He had the omnipotence
of God behind Him, why must He wait any longer for His
victory? Why this terribly disillusioning and heart-breaking
talk about suffering and rejection and the Cross?

It is not only His first disciples who have felt this to be
the most unwelcome part of Christ's teaching, for so it
has been felt in every age. "We preach Christ crucified,"
wrote St. Paul in the next generation, "unto the Jews a
stumbling-block, and unto the Greeks foolishness." The
Cross has ever been the stumbling-block. The Christian
religion would have aroused much less opposition in the
world if it had left out its emphasis on sorrow and suffering
and death and spoken to men only of life and joy and peace,
if it had offered men Easter and Whitsuntide without Lent
and Good Friday. But a religion that deliberately chooses
a gallows-tree for its coat-of-arms, what do men want with
that?

I am sure we ourselves often feel just as the disciples felt.
Sometimes when a Sunday morning dawns gloriously, when
all nature seems glad, when the whole world seems "bright

and beautiful and full of joy," we ask ourselves why we should go to Church and give ear to the austerities and so-brieties of this Christian teaching. Would it not be better to be out in the open, joining in nature's own chorus of praise, listening to the singing of the birds and gaily carol-ling with them, watching the gambolling of the lambs and disporting ourselves with a like lightness of heart? Why should we tread with Christ the *via dolorosa* on such a day as this? Surely the goal of life can be reached by a more cheerful road!

That is a mood to which none of us can claim to be complete strangers, but in many quarters it is now being elevated into an elaborate philosophy of life, sometimes even into a counter-religion that is placed in competition with the religion of the Cross. In Germany, for instance, during the Nazi era a determined effort was made to replace Christianity in the affections and hearts of the people by a new religion that had no sadness or tragedy in it but only the zest and joy of life. I have seen the bands of Hitler youth roam about the country-side of a Sunday morning, often assembling in the very square before the Church and at the very hour of morning service, so that the young men and maidens might be allured to follow them rather than join the congregation of the Christian faithful. Their motto, displayed on brightly-coloured banners, was "Strength through Joy." And they explicitly repudiated the Christian idea of joy through suffering. The Cross, you see, is still the stumbling-block.

What then is it that is lacking in this religion of natural joy? Why must we turn aside from the singing of the birds and the gambolling of the lambs, and engage in these solemn exercises of the Christian religion? Why these aus-terities and sobrieties? Why these prayers and fastings? Why these Lenten mournings? Why is the Cross necessary? Why did our Lord say that the Son of Man must first suffer?

The answer is quite clear. It is sin that makes it necessary. It is sin that introduces all the complications into the life of nature. It is sin that makes it impossible to rest content in a simple natural religion. It was sin that put the Cross into Christianity. It was sin that made it impossible for the Kingdom to come in the easy way that the disciples hoped. In a sinless world it might come that way, but not in a sinful world. The Son of Man had first to suffer—that was what the disciples came at last to understand.

> The grief and bitter passion
> Were all for sinners' gain;
> Mine, mine was the transgression,
> But thine the deadly pain.

The fact is that sometimes when we wake on such a glorious Sunday morning as I described, we really forget for a moment that the earth is not still a Garden of Eden. We forget that we are not as were Adam and Eve in the days of their innocence. The religion of the Hitler youth would have done not so badly for Adam and Eve in their primeval paradise. It was a natural religion, and the old theologians always taught that the religion of Adam and Eve was a natural religion. But when we try to recover that religion today, we are forgetting the Fall.

Now indeed I think that there are moments in life when we may forget the Fall. There are still in Scotland today, thank God, some places where God's world looks very much the same as it did before the Fall; by which I mean, not that I know anything about how Scotland looked at some remote period of the past, but that there are places in it today which are still unspoiled by the vandal hand of man. I can show you a little corner of paradise within an hour of my own door—a little spot where the earth is still a Garden of Eden. And in such a spot we can watch our children play in the same innocent and natural way as do the very lambs themselves. In hours and scenes of that kind there still lingers something of primeval innocence, something that sin has not spoiled, something of which we can say, as our Lord Himself said, that "of such is the Kingdom of Heaven." And I think it is right and good that we should delight in such hours and scenes and give a real place to them in our lives. For I am no puritan to look with peevish and suspicious eyes upon such natural gaiety. Rather do I say with Wordsworth,

> O evil day! if I were sullen
> While earth herself is adorning,
>   This sweet May morning
> And the children are culling
>   On every side,
> In a thousand valleys far and wide,
> Fresh flowers; while the sun shines warm,
> And the babe leaps up on his mother's arm.

Ah yes, but it doesn't last very long! Those golden hours are soon over! Perhaps the children themselves begin squabbling, giving way to passions that are not at all pretty or paradisal. Then memory soon returns to burden us, the memory of our own evil passions and evil deeds, our tarnished record, our smirched ideals, our neglected opportunities, our mismanaged human relationships. We return to the city to be met on all sides by evidences of a fallen world. We pass by the slums and the prisons. Overhead perhaps we hear the bombing aeroplanes, practising the arts of death. Everywhere around us are the signs of selfishness and greed and social injustice and the feud of rich and poor. Earth a paradise! The very suggestion is fraught with bitter irony, as in that story I once read of a foul London slum which boasted the name of Paradise Court, until we cry out in despair that there can never be any paradise again. And then perhaps we are ready to understand why the Son of Man must first suffer.

Look then into this a little more closely. The first thing to understand is that *there is no way out of sin except through suffering*. Sometimes we are inclined to grumble at this dispensation of things. We think it too bad that our sins should bring such dire consequences. We ask whether the omnipotent God could not have arranged things otherwise. And some men refuse to believe in God at all because He has not arranged things otherwise. But what then would they have? Would they prefer that sin should produce happiness? Would they prefer that sinners should prosper? Would they prefer that wickedness should go scot-free? Would they prefer that greed and licence and hatred should bring rewards instead of punishments? Surely rather we must agree with the fine words of James Martineau, "Sin being there, it would be simply monstrous that there should be no suffering, and would fully justify the despair which raises its sickly cry of complaint against the retributory wretchedness of human transgression."

Of course, if pleasure were the chief end of man, then indeed it would have been better if God had designed a world where sin did not involve suffering. The world would then be a fine amusement park. Aye, but it would be a very poor school. It would be a hopelessly bad training ground. It would never lead men to holiness. It would never lead them to glorify God and enjoy Him forever, and if we believe that *that* is the chief end of man I think we can see that the sequence of sin and suffering is a wise dispensation on the part of One who loves us well.

But now the second thing to understand is that *our own suffering is not enough*. Our sin leads to suffering, and it is right that it should do so. Yet no man has ever reached the

point when he has felt that his sufferings have atoned for
his sins. However long a weird some of us may have to dree,
we never feel that we have washed ourselves clean or have
undone the past or have made our reparation.

> Could my tears for ever flow,
> All for sin could not atone.

So the end would still be death, as in the old Greek tragedies; and the Kingdom of God would still tarry. Aye, and
if we had had the doing of it, it would tarry for ever and a
day. But, thank God, we have not had the doing of it.
Thank God that in His love and in His pity He has taken
the doing of it upon Himself. His holy Son has suffered for
our sakes and in our stead. The Kingdom is indeed assured
to us, as much assured as if we had never sinned. Paradise
is regained, as certainly regained as if it had never been lost.
But the Son of Man had first to suffer.

What now about your own sin? Is there something that
is weighing a little on your mind today? Something you did
long ago perhaps, and about which you have never found
peace. Something you did, or omitted to do, last week?
Some little dishonesty? Some little unchastity? Some nasty
little meanness you practised on somebody? Some hard,
uncharitable word you spoke at the breakfast-table this
morning, and the memory of which still rankles in your
heart and another's? It may seem a very small thing, a pec-
cadillo rather than a sin. In itself it was a small thing—a
single word, a single look, a moment's lapse only. Yet who
can measure its results? The terrible thing about sin is the
rapidity with which it spreads its ravages from even the
smallest beginnings. The smallest untruth, for instance, will
soon need another to back it up, and then another, and
another. "Lying," says an old eighteenth-century book, "is
like a wild, huge, irregular Forest; where you will be hard

put to it, unless you have a strong Memory indeed, to re-member the place of any particular Tree you have mark'd. Truth, on the other hand, is a small regular Enclosure, where you can easily go again to anything you have once seen." How true that is! And moreover, to what an infinity of suffering does the smallest sin often lead! It was only a momentary lapse, you say. Yes, but it put God's world out of joint! Only a single word, but it was broadcast to the stars! "I strike a stone, and the shock is felt in Neptune." Had that little sin of yours been the only sin ever com-mitted, it alone would have been enough to start the miser-able ball rolling. It alone would have been enough to make an end of the Garden of Eden. It alone would have been enough to bring "death into the world and all our woe." Wasn't the old story right in supposing that the eating of a single forbidden apple was enough in itself to cause the irretrievable disaster?

Is there then any way out for you? Is there any way back? Yes, there is a way; but it passes through the sufferings of Christ. For that one little sin of yours Christ must die. With that one word, with that one look, you crucified Him. Yes, in spite of what you have done, the Kingdom of Heaven may still come for you. But the Son of Man must first suffer.

Or again, consider the dreadful state of the world at the present moment. What a scene of turmoil it is, and of bitter strife! What a cockpit of ugly passions and murderous hatreds! Nation lifting up its hand against nation, and brother against brother! Ploughshares being turned with diabolical rapidity and ingenuity into swords, and pruning-hooks into spears! Here again, the fatal ball has started to roll. Here again sin leads on to sin in that vicious circle of which the present competition in armaments is a sort of symbolic expression. The end of such things can only be death.

Is there any way out, then? Can the fond hope of a better world ever be realised? Shall we ever enjoy the promised reign of righteousness and peace of which all the prophets dreamed? Yes it may come and shall come, but not by any easy road. Not by any painless process of education. Not by any natural evolution. Not by any gradual and easy progress. All the facts give the lie to such utopian dreams. There is no way but the *via dolorosa*. Please God, these things shall be!—but they can only be through the Cross. "For as the lightning, that lighteneth out of the one part under heaven, shineth unto the other part under heaven; so shall also the Son of Man be in his day. But first must he suffer many things." Each new international quarrel adds to His sufferings. Every taunt that one nation casts at another increases His stripes. Every fresh piece of lying propaganda drives another nail into His wounds. Every new bombing aeroplane that is built adds another pang to His grief. There is no other way than the way that leads over Calvary.

Let us then thank God for His unspeakable gift. Let us thank Him for the sufferings of Him by whose stripes we can alone be healed. Let us thank Him that at the very centre of our religion there stands a Cross. And let us take good heed that we do not now, after hearing all this, go out into the world proposing to crucify our Lord afresh.

20

NONE OTHER NAME

Neither is there salvation in any other: for there is none other name under heaven given among men, whereby we must be saved.   ACTS IV, 12.

THESE words, spoken by St. Peter before the Jewish supreme court within a few weeks or months of Jesus' death, may seem to put the Christian claim at its very highest, and yet it is doubtful whether the claim would be worth making at all, if it were pitched any lower. When so much is said, we may perhaps be perplexed; but if less were said, we should hardly be interested.

What is claimed is that there is no hope of salvation for the world or for any one in it save in Jesus Christ. If it be asked what is meant by salvation, I would quote the opening words of a book by the philosopher Bernard Bosanquet:

"What must I do to be saved?" The old monosyllable, which since the coming of Christ has sounded so clearly the S.O.S. call of humanity, utters, it would seem, an ultimate need. And yet what is it? Saved from what? The old word does not say; and this, I think, is very significant. We are to understand without telling, and I suppose we do.

Yes, I suppose we do. We know that the world is sick and needs to be made whole. We know that the world is in deadly peril and needs to be made safe. We know that the world is all wrong and needs to be put right. The story of world religion in every age and every land is the story of an ardent and tireless and even desperate quest of salvation. We Christians cannot for a moment claim that we have been more diligent than others in the quest. If we are tempted to think so, a visit to the banks of the Ganges or to the shores of the Red Sea will swiftly disillusion us. And if we have found in Christ that which all men have sought, is it not rather that He has found us? If He should say to us, "I was found of them that sought me not," what is there that we can reply?

But what our modern minds sometimes stumble at is the exclusiveness of this Christian claim. That some have found salvation in Jesus Christ is not to be denied; but that there is none other name in which anybody anywhere can find salvation—that may seem to say too much. This is what has been called "the scandal of particularity." The word scandal means stumbling-block, and no doubt here is a stumbling-block for many minds. A German philosopher of the Enlightenment expressed his protest by saying that "The Godhead loves not to pour His whole essence into a single instance." Why, it is asked, should there not be several ways of salvation, or several different mediators of a single way? Why should God choose to reveal His fulness through only one historical figure, to only one people, and in only one age of the world's history? And especially *that* figure and *that* people and *that* age!

> How odd
> Of God
> To choose
> The Jews!

Why should He elect that little land of Palestine, that obscure backwater within the great Roman Empire, which has been as a thorn in the side of all who have tried to administer it from that day to this? And that backwater provincial people so little versed in the higher arts of civilization? And then from among them all, a village carpenter's son?

Well, there are two things I would like to say about this.

First, when we ask ourselves why these things should be, we have to answer simply that we do not know. We have to take experience as we find it. We have to take history as we find it. We have to take truth as we find it. And above all we have to accept the action of God as we discover it to be. We cannot pretend to know in advance how God ought to act for the enlightenment and salvation of the human race. We are not in a position to lay down conditions. So when the German philosopher tells me that, "The Godhead loves not to pour His whole essence into a single instance," I cannot but wonder how he knows this. In a letter to his friend M. de Beaumont, Rousseau once asked, "Is it simple, is it natural, that God should have gone and found Moses in order to speak to Jean Jacques Rousseau?" Well, I admit it is not simple; but what right have we to assume that truth is simple or that God governs His universe on a simple plan? And as to whether it is natural, have we any knowledge of what would be natural in such a region of experience apart from the witness of the experience itself? If we believe in God at all—and if we do not, this whole question loses its meaning—then we must allow Him to bring His salvation to us in ways of His own choosing, and it will indeed be surprising if these are not very different from anything that we, with our limited wisdom and intelligence, could have foreseen. The private soldier can never expect to have much insight into the strategy of a great campaign.

So when we ask ourselves why it should be ordained that there is only one Name whereby we all must be saved, our first answer is that, if we do not know why, we do not need to know and could hardly expect to know. And yet—this is my second point—I believe we can say a little more than that. We could not be wise before the event, but perhaps we can be a little wiser after it. Perhaps the event itself has enlightened us, so that we can now see something of the reason why things should stand thus. Is it not contained in Christ's own word, "that they all may be one"? That, you remember, was His prayer to the Father before He crossed the brook Cedron into the Garden of Gethsemane on the eve of His crucifixion: "That they all may be one; as thou, Father, art in me, and I in thee, that they also may be one in us . . . And the glory which thou gavest me, I have given them, that they may be one, even as we are one; I in them, and thou in me, that they may be made perfect in one." If it had been so that each could find God in his own way, then each would be finding Him without at the same time finding his brother. If the love of God were revealed to each in a different place, then we could all love Him without meeting one another in love. If the various tribes of mankind could find salvation in different names, then the human race would forever be divided. Men might still attempt to unite on the level of certain secondary and prudential interests, but are we not learning today by bitter experience how fragile and unstable this kind of association must always be, if in their ultimate concern, which is the concern for salvation, men remain apart? Modern science has given us a magnificent lead in the endeavour to transcend all boundaries of race and nation and colour and language, but it is becoming clearer every day that this will avail us little until we are of one mind about the ultimate good which our science should be made to serve.

Was it not then a gracious ordering of things on God's part that there should be salvation in one Name only; that we can meet with Him only by meeting with one another;

by betaking ourselves all together to one place—to one "green hill far away, without the city wall"; by encountering there a single figure to whom we all together give our whole allegiance; by listening to the self-same story; by reading in the same Holy Book; by being baptized in the same Name into the same fellowship; by eating and drinking at the same Holy Table—"all made to drink [as St. Paul says] into one Spirit"; so that [as he also says] "there is no difference between the Jew and the Greek; for the same Lord over all is rich unto all them that call upon him"; and Jew and Greek, Barbarian, Scythian, bondman and freeman are all one in Him? "He is our peace," says St. Paul once more—and how the world today longs for peace! "He is our peace, who hath made both one, and hath broken down the middle wall of partition between us." Perhaps if for "middle wall of partition" we read "iron curtain" or "bamboo curtain" we understand a little more of what St. Paul had in mind, and can enter more deeply into his burning zeal for the propagation of a gospel which should transcend all differences of race and tongue and tribe and nation—with "one body, and one Spirit . . . , one Lord, one faith, one baptism, one God and Father of all, who is above all, and through all, and in you all."

21

THE RESURRECTION

And we are witnesses of all things which he did both in the land of the Jews, and in Jerusalem; whom they slew and hanged on a tree: Him God raised up the third day, and shewed him openly; not to all the people, but unto witnesses chosen before of God, even to us, who did eat and drink with him after he rose from the dead. And he commanded us to preach to the people, and to testify that it is he who was ordained of God to be the judge of quick and dead. To him give all the prophets witness, that through his name whosoever believeth in him shall receive remission of sins. ACTS X, 39–43.

THAT is part of the sermon that St. Peter preached before the household of Cornelius. And in it he puts the whole Gospel in a nutshell. So much so indeed that when the Apostles' Creed was afterwards formulated as a convenient short statement of the faith, those who composed it drew very largely on this sermon of St. Peter's. It tells "how God anointed Jesus of Nazareth with the Holy Spirit and with power: who went about doing good, and healing all that were oppressed by the devil; . . . how they slew him and hanged him on a tree: Him God raised up the third day, and shewed him openly; how it is he who was ordained of God to be the judge of quick and dead; and how through his name whosoever believeth in him shall receive remission of sins."

But now, if St. Peter had said no more than that, one can imagine that the household of Cornelius might very well ask, "How are we to know whether all these things are true? It is all very well to affirm these things; but how are we to believe them?" To that question St. Peter had a threefold reply, and it is that reply that I want to explain to you.

The first part of St. Peter's reply is this: "We are witnesses of all things which he did both in the land of the Jews, and in Jerusalem: we ourselves saw him slain and crucified; and we were witnesses also of his resurrection: when he rose from the dead, God shewed him openly, not indeed to all the people, but to witnesses chosen in advance, *even to us*, who did eat and drink with him after he rose from the dead."

What an impression that reply must have made on the household of Cornelius! We cannot be at all surprised that the next verse goes on to say, "While Peter yet spake these words, the Holy Ghost fell on all them which heard the word." To be actually standing in the presence of one who had himself touched and handled the Word of Life, who had walked the Galilean ways in Jesus' company, who had strolled through the cornfields with Him, and sat with Him on the hill-sides, who had looked into His eyes and seen His lips actually form the words, when he spoke the parables of the Prodigal Son and the Good Samaritan; who had been with Him in Gethsemane and at each of the Stations of the *via dolorosa*; who had seen Him crucified, and watched the life ebb from His broken body as He spoke the seven words from the Cross! And, above all, to be standing in the presence of one who had seen Him and spoken with Him, and even eaten and drunk with Him, after He had risen from the dead! No wonder the Holy Ghost fell on all who heard Him, and that they all believed. We feel, perhaps, that if we had been present in that house in Caesarea that day, the effect on us would have been the same. Or we feel that if an eye-witness to the things that were done in Judaea and in Jerusalem, and especially an eye-witness to the Resurrection, were to appear in Edinburgh this Easter morning, and should be able to say, as he preached the Gospel to us, "I actually *saw* the Lord Christ after He rose from the dead, and actually *spoke* to Him and actually *touched* Him, and even *had a meal* with Him," then *everybody* in Edinburgh would believe, and become His devoted followers, and not just a few, as it is today. And yet, without at all seeking to minimise the immensely blessed privilege of that first generation of Christians, who stood at only one remove from the actual events themselves, I take leave to doubt whether they had as great an advantage over ourselves as all that. For after all, though the whole household of Cornelius believed, there were a great many who heard St. Peter preach in Caesarea and elsewhere who did not believe. And suppose such a thing could happen as that one of the eye-witnesses of our Lord's resurrection should appear in Edinburgh today, and say that he had eaten and drunk with the risen Lord, what do you think would be the result? We know what it would be. Some would say he was deliberately lying. Others would say that he had somehow been deceived, that he had been the victim either of imposture or of self-delusion. Still others would just not be interested, and would turn him away. And I believe that even the most sympathetic people would be sceptical, unless the speaker could produce some other proof or evidence than his mere verbal statement. They would not want merely to take his word for it that the things he said were true. Indeed I should say the same even of the household of Cornelius itself. I don't believe they were willing merely to take the word of this lodger in the tanner's house on the Joppa sea-shore, that Jesus Christ was risen from the dead. They wanted something more.

And they had got something more. St. Peter gave them something more than his bare word. And so I come to *my second head*. For St. Peter said not only "We are witnesses," but he said (v. 43), "To him give all the prophets witness." That is to say St. Peter substantiated his claims for his Lord, not only by bearing his own testimony as an eye-witness to the life, passion, death and resurrection of Jesus, but also by an appeal to the whole Old Testament revelation. He knew that the events which had so recently transpired in Galilee and Jerusalem could not be properly and believingly understood except in the light, and in the context, of all that had gone before—ever since Abraham went out not knowing whither he went, ever since Moses led his people through the wilderness into the promised land. Had not Jesus Himself said that very thing: "If ye hear not Moses and the prophets, neither will ye be persuaded though one should rise from the dead." These solemn words should in themselves be enough to convince us of the importance for our faith of the Old Testament scriptures. There has been some tendency in our time to neglect the Old Testament in favour only of the New. There are those who say that the New Testament speaks to their need, but that they can manage well without most of the Old. But they who speak thus speak foolishly. Jesus Himself spoke of His Gospel as the fulfilment of that more ancient revelation, and how can we understand the fulfilment unless we understand that which in the fulfilment is being fulfilled? That is why the evangelists connect every incident in the Gospel story with something in the earlier story of the Hebrew people, or with some word spoken by the prophets. Such and such a thing happened, they say, "that the Scriptures must be ful-filled." And that is why St. Peter was careful to add the testimony of the prophets to his own testimony as an eye-witness; saying not only, "We are his witnesses" but also, "To him bear all the prophets witness."

But do you think St. Peter gave no other witness to the household of Cornelius besides these two? I am sure he did; and so I come to my third and last head. For what after all was it that persuaded the household of Cornelius to believe what Peter told them of Christ, and especially—that most difficult thing—what he had told them of His resurrection? When he said he had actually spoken and eaten with Jesus after His resurrection, that was undoubtedly impressive, but not by itself convincing—for he might have been deceived. When he expounded to them those passages in the ancient prophets that pointed forward to this resurrection, that undoubtedly added great weight to his testimony, but again it did not in itself absolutely clinch the matter; for how were they to be sure that this man of Nazareth was the person to whom all these prophecies applied? No, some extra thing was needed, and Peter gave it to them. For he not only affirmed that Jesus had risen from the dead, but he gave them convincing evidence that *He was still alive.*

Read that wonderful story of Cornelius again (Acts x), and ask yourself what it really was that converted that household. Cornelius was a Roman from Italy, living in the land of the Jews as a captain in the local regiment of the occupying Roman army. But during his long stay in Judaea he had come under the influence of the Jewish religion and the Old Testament revelation. We are told (v. 22) that he was "a just man, and one that feareth God, and of good report among all the nation of the Jews." But after all he was a Gentile, he was not of the seed of Abraham; and therefore the Jews had refused to accept him or to grant him the privileges and blessings of their holy religion. But when St. Peter came to him, things were quite different. The

Jews had shut him out, but St. Peter took him in—and all his Roman household with him. "Ye know," St. Peter said, "how that it is an unlawful thing for a man that is a Jew to keep company or come unto one of another nation; but God hath shewed me that I should not call any man common or unclean. . . . Can any man forbid water, that these should not be baptized, which have received the Holy Ghost as well as we?"

Now I would put it to you that those who heard St. Peter speak these words, and those who saw him take action in accordance with them, were thereby enabled really to believe in the Risen Lord. They believed in the Resurrection, not merely because the prophets had foretold it, and because St. Peter had affirmed it, but because by his conduct among them, and his attitude towards them, he provided direct evidence that Jesus was still alive. They could see now that there was a new force at work in the world—at work in the heart of St. Peter and of the young Christian Church. That was what converted the household of Cornelius. They believed on the Lord Jesus Christ, not just because Peter said He had risen, but because Peter showed them that He was still alive and still at work in His Church.

Now it is in this third sense that you and I are called upon today to be witnesses to our Lord's Resurrection. We have not the privilege that Peter had of being *eye*-witnesses of the Resurrection. We cannot testify, as he could, that we have eaten and drunk with Him after He rose from the dead. But we *can*, by our behaviour and by our whole walk and conversation, bear witness that He still lives. We can show that His gracious Spirit is still as active as ever it was during the days of His flesh. We can show that His love is still a power in the world. And unless we bear this living witness, no other witness that we bear can be of much effect. Men will never believe that the things we say about Jesus Christ are true, unless we show them how that truth works out in practice in our own lives. Men will not even understand what we mean by the love of Christ, unless we give them an object lesson, in our own action and behaviour, of what that love means when translated into practical terms in the relation of man to man. This is what is so much emphasized in I John. We know that we have

passed from death unto life, because we love the brethren. . . . But whoso hath this world's good, and seeth his brother have need, and shutteth up his bowels of compassion for him, how dwelleth the love of God in him? . . . No man hath seen God at any time. If we love one another, God dwelleth in us, and his love is perfected in us.

If we look back on the whole long story of the Christian mission, and ask what it was that really brought men into the Christian Church, I think we shall have to say that it was never just preaching, or the unsupported witness of words. The men of all ages and of all nations have not been drawn into the Christian Church, just because a man stood up before them and recited to them the truths of the Creed. Men have been drawn to Christ because they saw His spirit at work in the world, because they found a new and wonderful thing at work in the life of the Christian community. The witness of Christian life has at all times been a necessary commentary on Gospel truth, a commentary necessary both to its understanding and to its acceptance. Why, for instance, am I myself a member of the Christian Church? What was it that drew me? It was never the bare recital of the things that took place long ago in Galilee and Jerusalem; it was rather because the life of the Christian home into which I was born convinced me that these things were true. I knew that Christ had risen from the dead, because I saw Him at work in the lives of my father and mother.

Let me give you one more example. St. Peter, who was a Jew, brought the Gospel to Cornelius who was a Gentile. But nowadays we of the Church of Scotland have a mission to the Jews themselves. That mission has been working among the Jews for several generations. But with notably small result. Very few Jews had been persuaded to believe. From early youth they had been brought up to regard Jesus Christ as the scandal and stumbling-block, and so they had developed inhibitions against the acceptance of the Christian Gospel that proved too strong to be overborne. *But* in the years preceding the recent war these Jews had been hunted and persecuted in one country of Europe after another; and in these days of their great need the principal help they received was from the Christian Church. And I have heard some of our missionaries among the Jews testify that this practical demonstration of Christian love did more for the conversion of these Jews to Christianity than all their previous preaching. I myself personally know some Jews who have in this way been drawn into the Christian Church. They understood at last what the love of Christ meant, when they saw it actualised in the hearts and lives of His disciples. They believed that the Lord had risen when they thus had experience of His risen power.

And this is the witness that we can all bear to the Resurrection—the most effective witness of all. Are we bearing this testimony? Is the life of our Christian community such that men will know, by looking at us, and by seeing how we behave, that our Lord has indeed risen from the dead, and liveth evermore? Why is it that in our day men are not being drawn into the Christian Church as they were drawn in days gone by? Can part of the reason be that we are not bearing this witness, as our fathers bore it?

WRITINGS OF JOHN BAILLIE

The Roots of Religion in the Human Soul (New York: Doran; London: Hodder & Stoughton, 1926)

The Interpretation of Religion (New York: Charles Scribner's Sons, 1928; Edinburgh: T. & T. Clark, 1929)

The Place of Jesus Christ in Modern Christianity (New York: Charles Scribner's Sons; Edinburgh: T. & T. Clark, 1929)

And the Life Everlasting (New York: Charles Scribner's Sons, 1933; London: Oxford University Press, 1934)

A Diary of Private Prayer (New York, Charles Scribner's Sons; London: Oxford University Press, 1937)

Our Knowledge of God (New York: Charles Scribner's Sons; London: Oxford University Press, 1939)

Invitation to Pilgrimage (New York: Charles Scribner's Sons; London: Oxford University Press, 1942)

The Prospects of Spiritual Renewal (London: Oxford University Press, 1943)

What is Christian Civilization? (New York: Charles Scribner's Sons; London: Christophers, 1945)

The Mind of the Modern University (University Pamphlets Series, London: S.C.M. Press, 1946)

Spiritual Religion (London: Allen & Unwin, n.d. [? 1947])

The Belief in Progress (New York: Charles Scribner's Sons; London: Oxford University Press, 1950)

The Human Situation (William Ainslie Memorial Lecture, London: Longmans, Green & Co. 1950)

Natural Science and the Spiritual Life (British Association Lecture, New York: Charles Scribner's Sons, 1952; London: Oxford University Press, 1951)

A Diary of Readings (edited, New York: Charles Scribner's Sons; London: Oxford University Press, 1955)

The Idea of Revelation in Recent Thought (New York: Columbia University Press; London: Oxford University Press, 1956)

POSTHUMOUSLY PUBLISHED:

The Sense of the Presence of God (Gifford Lectures for 1961–62. New York: Charles Scribner's Sons, London: Oxford University Press, 1962)

Christian Devotion (New York: Charles Scribner's Sons; London: Oxford University Press, 1962)

A Reasoned Faith (New York: Charles Scribner's Sons; London: Oxford University Press, 1963)

INDEX

INDEX

179